Sir Yehudi Menuhin is probably the world's most famous living musician, loved and respected not only for his extraordinary achievement in the world of music but also as a man of great wisdom and integrity.

On 22 April 1991, Sir Yehudi is seventy-five years old. These conversations, on a wide range of topics, celebrate the man, his music and his personal philosophy. The conversations with musicologist David Dubal took place on a number of occasions and in various locations, from private meetings to open platform performances at the Juilliard School. The discussion ranged broadly over many subjects, from music, musicians and composers, to politics, art, religion, culture and the environment, conversations which David Dubal has now collected into this volume.

Offering unique insights into the life and mind of one of the most remarkable figures in twentieth-century music, this book is a fitting celebration of the man.

Conversations with Menuhin

Also by David Dubal:

The World Of The Concert Pianist
The Art Of The Piano

Conversations with Menuhin

A Celebration On His 75th Birthday

 by DAVID DUBAL

(1991)

HEINEMANN : LONDON

David Dubal is the author of *The World Of The Concert Pianist* and *The Art Of The Piano*. He is a concert pianist, broadcaster, and has been on the faculty of the Juilliard School since 1983, where he teaches Piano Literature. For two decades, he was Music Director of New York City's classical music station WNCN. His six-part radio series, *Conversations with Horowitz*, won the George Foster Peabody Award. A Steinway Artist, David Dubal has performed and lectured extensively. He has given master classes, and has been a judge at international piano competitions. He lives in New York City.

For Carol Bresner

William Heinemann Limited
Michelin House, 81 Fulham Road, London SW3 6RB

LONDON   MELBOURNE   AUCKLAND

First published in Great Britain 1991
Copyright © David Dubal 1991

A CIP catalogue record for this book
is available from the British Library

ISBN 0 434 21674 7

Typeset by Hewer Text Composition Services, Edinburgh
Printed in Great Britain by Clays Ltd., St. Ives plc.

ACKNOWLEDGEMENTS

My thanks to Agnes Bruneau for bringing Yehudi Menuhin to me. To Nadia Lawrence, my editor at Heinemann, for her skill and goodwill. To Kenneth Bookstein for saving several badly recorded tapes. To Hilde Limondjian, Director of Concerts and Lectures at the Metropolitan Museum of Art, who arranged for Menuhin and myself to appear at the Grace Rainey Rogers auditorium. And my gratitude to Eri Ikezi for special care in the preparation of the typescript as well as her many valuable suggestions.

David Dubal, 1991

Preface

On a winter's morning, while sitting at my desk at Radio
Station WNCN preparing some work for the day, I spied a
batch of records not put back on their shelf. On top was the
Elgar Violin Concerto with Yehudi Menuhin and Sir Adrian
Boult conducting. I remembered this performance as particularly fine, and had not heard it in some time. I was precisely
in the mood to hear it, and soon I found myself spellbound by
Menuhin's playing of the angelic slow movement. It is playing possessed of that romantic intensity peculiar to Menuhin
at his best.

The rude ring of the telephone shook me from my divine
reverie. It was the bright voice of Agnes Bruneau – one of
New York's best music publicists.

'David,' she said, 'how would you like to talk with Sir
Yehudi Menuhin, who will be in New York only on Thursday?
He would love talking to you. Perhaps you could interview
him and do a programme with him.'

I forgot to tell Agnes that at that very moment I was listening to Menuhin; instead, I blithely replied, 'Agnes, I just
can't do it Thursday. It's impossible, I'm busy every hour.'

'Well, what a pity,' she said, with the utter dejection
that only a PR person can muster up. 'I guess some other
time.'

As I turned back to the record player to raise the volume,
Menuhin was closing the slow movement, and a phrase of
Baudelaire's entered my head: 'Suddenly there vibrates
in your ears a *dying* air executed by the rapturous bow of
Paganini.' This strange fragment somehow brought me to

my senses, and I said to myself, 'Menuhin will be here Thursday and I have *no time to talk to him?*'

In a flash, I called Agnes and told her to bring Mr Menuhin on Thursday. Happily she said, 'He'll come directly from the airport. He will be here at two.'

On Thursday, the whole staff was excited. Many musical celebrities had been to the station, of course, but Menuhin was a legend of the musical world, and everybody wanted to shake his hand.

Exactly on time, he arrived. He was graciousness personified. He showed no sign of fatigue from his transatlantic flight. Before our interview, he casually submitted, for probably the millionth time, to the giving of autographs, signing record albums and being photographed – all of this with an easy charm and a resigned patience.

We then proceeded to the recording studio. Usually, this procedure took a little more than an hour. Just enough time to create a programme which included music. But as the hour passed, I realized that this would not be my usual talk. One hour became two hours, and soon three hours became five hours. Here was that rarity, a musician born to express ideas as well as music. During this time, quite a little audience had gathered behind us in the studio to listen to him. I listened intently, hoping to keep my questions coming.

During this long time, Menuhin never left his seat, and although he was brought some yogurt, it was hardly touched. He was happy to talk; it seemed important to him to bring forth his ideas. Expressing himself appeared essential to his nature, even a responsibility. After five hours, he was not even slightly weary.

Afterwards, I invited him to dinner, but he declined. He wanted to go to his hotel and call his wife, Diana, who he said would be worried about him. He was delighted with the interview and exclaimed softly, 'You are my Boswell – you have brought out all new material. Perhaps we should make a little book from it.' And that sentence was the genesis of the present volume. Although his schedule was fearsome, we made plans to see each other again to continue our talks. And so we did on various occasions throughout three years, sometimes for an hour or so in hotel rooms in Washington and New York, or on the stage of the Metropolitan Museum in front of an audience.

Menuhin's life has been a journey of unusual fulfilment. He has travelled the globe on a magic carpet with his violin as his magic wand. With this instrument, he has charmed and moved perhaps more people than any violinist in history. His career has been monumental. His name has been a household word from childhood. Seldom, if ever, has a child survived so well the perils of prodigy-hood and succeeded so prodigiously in adulthood. His very persona, the chiselled expressiveness of his face, the look of devotional inspiration, presents to the public the old nineteenth-century image of the great musician as a romantic and spiritual guide.

Since the horrors of Nazi Germany, the arts have had to withstand an unbearable fall in prestige. We now know that being an artist does not hold the monster back. Yet we collectively suffer desperately from losing a perhaps naïve but, nonetheless, idealistic notion of the artist as humanity's great representative, its pride and joy. As a human family, are we not proudest of Leonardo, Michelangelo, Beethoven and other giants of the arts? Are these artists not humankind's mirror of transcendence? Today, there are fewer great artists that symbolize to the public the artist as visionary and humanist. Menuhin is one of the last of these musicians of great elevation, who can inspire many people with the healing and spiritual qualities of art. He is of the philosophical line which produced Liszt, Busoni, Paderewski, Albert Schweitzer and Georges Enesco – Menuhin's own teacher.

Menuhin's art is not a self-absorbed devouring demon. It

is part of life. As well as having an endless curiosity about music and a hunger to play it, for him music is pure love. Menuhin is the antithesis of the stereotyped image of the artist as at least 'half mad'. He proves that an artist need not be a neurotic. Indeed, that art is more wonderful when it is part of a healthy personality. Menuhin is a healthy man, and herein lies his greatness as well as his worldly success. He cares for his own physical being; he feels a moral commitment to those near him, be they his concert audience or his family. And he is poignantly aware that we live on a divided and deteriorating planet.

Menuhin also has learned the greatest of all secrets – how to use time. He lives on a different time cycle than most others. For him life has not been a mere seventy-five years. Such a triumph is only achieved by the most serious people. Thus he is able to sow many seeds. As Laurence Durrell wrote, 'Menuhin's eager pleading on behalf of man's nobler part puts to shame the tepid hearts and shrinking souls among us. Never has a busy public man responded to so many claims on his time or crammed his spare moments with such diverse activities.'

Menuhin's curiosity is indefatigable. As he says in the course of this text, 'I want to understand every phenomenon in the world.' Glenn Gould once asked Menuhin to visit 'the outpost communities of Arctic Canada'. Gould wrote, 'I have no doubt that he will return with a trunkful of ethnographic tabulations, the sketch for an improved system of Eskimo shorthand, and the manuscript of a lecture detailing the nutritional deficiencies of the barren-ground caribou.'

Of course, it is as a master violinist that Menuhin's name will live. Quite a large number of his output of recordings will remain treasures of the violinist's art. As an interpreter, he has the rare gift of completely giving himself to the composition at hand and, with it, the ability to commune with his listener, making him or her a part of the performance. Nadia

Boulanger described a Menuhin recital: 'An altogether superb concert. He gave a number of encores, and the last was the slow movement of Brahms' Sonata in D minor. What happened then was part of an indescribable completeness. The whole house found itself in the grip of the same mute emotion, which created silence of an extraordinary quality. Everyone understood, felt, participated in what he himself must have been feeling . . .'

Menuhin possessed this quality from childhood. Even then, his playing went beyond mature interpretation. It was an innate innocence (which is still intact) that made Einstein declare that, hearing the boy, he now knew there was a God.

I cannot refrain from including one other tribute, this one by George Steiner: 'Menuhin's radiance is tangible to anyone near him, but also to those who crowd the furthest row of a concert hall. The fineness of his features, the economy and elegance of gesture which surround his performance are important, of course. But the force lies much deeper. Menuhin has made of the music he produces a total expression and embodiment of being. To hear him play the Bartók solo Sonata, or the Elgar Concerto, even at a distance or on a worn record, is to be asked, in a peculiarly intimate, directly focussed way, into his complete presence. It is a presence that seems to encounter the world and oneself with a sovereign courtesy of heart.'

Menuhin at seventy-five is a physical marvel – lean, immaculate and elegant in dress. He is refined but never rarefied. His voice is cultivated and agreeable in timbre. His manners are impeccable; his courtesy contagious. He is totally at ease with himself, and he listens intensely to others. It would be impossible for him to have any condescension for the less superior of the species. He is open to every topic, and is extremely easy to be with.

Menuhin is at his happiest when he is with his wife, Diana,

a person of dazzling intellect and conversational brilliance. With her, he responds with every fibre of his being. There can be nothing so delightful as dining with them. Together, they possess a natural abundance and quiet energy, which is unique in my experience.

Menuhin at seventy-five is thriving; still giving to the world with an unstinting energy. He has always been the host in life. To have merely been a guest would have been unthinkable for him. For his seventy-fifth birthday, I present this volume.

David Dubal

PART ONE

On Music and Musicians

Dubal: What is it in Bach's music that makes it so transcendent? It must surely be more than his magnificent musical logic.

Menuhin: Bach is a mystic; he has a union with the divine, or at least identification with the cosmos, with the universe, with the infinite. That is a state of being which Bach can create.

Dubal: Do you think Bach consciously felt this 'divine union'?

Menuhin: He was simply extremely devout; he was a believer.

Dubal: Your statement reminds me of someone asking Haydn why his masses were so joyful and indeed almost jovial, and Haydn replied, 'Because whenever I think of God, I always feel so indescribably happy.' When this anecdote was told to Goethe, tears poured down his cheeks.

Menuhin: I think today we can also be believers without necessarily believing the strict doctrine of any church. But we can still have that feeling. And what moves us, apart from the structure, or the mathematics – because structure is a kind of frozen mathematics – is the grandeur and the fullness and balance of Bach's music. It possesses a perfect mental and emotional balance. Nor is it Bach's ego that is speaking. He represents something greater within us that unites us to our fellow men rather than separates us from our fellow men.

Dubal: I'm fond of your Beethoven recordings you made with Kempff – such a pure and rare artist.

Kempff

Menuhin: Oh, yes, yes. He really was, of all the pianists I've played with, the one closest to Beethoven in the sense that one had the feeling that Beethoven was one of his old friends. And he could take little liberties and Beethoven would say to him, 'Oh, that's fine, go right ahead, my friend.' There was an intimacy in his handling Beethoven which was quite revealing, and that is an assurance many young people lack. Because they revere him and worship him, and quite rightly, but they don't know how to treat him as a friend who is alive.

Dubal: They give him an autopsy.

Menuhin: Yes, exactly. Or they treat him, although playing it very beautifully, good tone and everything else, cleanly, but it doesn't mean anything. But if you really spent your life as Kempff did with Beethoven, then everything took on its real meaning.

Dubal: Your late brother-in-law, the eminent pianist Louis Kentner, once said that Beethoven was the greatest artist in human civilization. What has Beethoven been to you? Has he been more than Bach, more than Mozart?

Menuhin: Of course, it's so hard to compare. I think I understand Beethoven, especially in his sonatas and symphonies. And I'd like to get to know his late string quartets better. That is a special world the way Beethoven grew in those late quartets. Perhaps fifty years ago, I wouldn't have hesitated. I think I would have said Beethoven meant more to me than any other. But life has brought other kinds of music, great music and great composers. I don't necessarily put them on the same level, but I couldn't live without them. I cannot live without Bartók, Mozart or Bach. Or Schubert. And so much else.

Dubal: What do you think Beethoven's relationship to the

violin was? We know much more about his relationship to the piano.

Menuhin: Well, I think he's basically a composer for the piano.

Dubal: Pianists have often said that Beethoven is pianistically awkward. How is he violinistically? How does it feel to practise the Concerto and the ten sonatas?

Menuhin: They're not awkward, but they're music first and violin playing later. I find Beethoven's music in a way more symbolic than anything else. It's not, in other words, of flesh and blood. It has a message each time. By symbolic I mean that the passages are not just scales and arpeggii, which they tend to look like.

Dubal: They surely look like Czerny exercises on the paper.

Menuhin: Exactly. And unless you can see them in their spiritual and symbolic implication, you've missed the point.

Dubal: I know you feel close to Brahms.

Menuhin: Enesco so loved Brahms – Brahms was the best-educated musician of his day. He followed no fashion. He was a late Romantic, who had the intellectual power to continue to infuse power into the sonata form. And he had a special vein of tenderness. I think he must have loved children – I say that because his tenderness has that ineffable quality.

Dubal: That's interesting you say that, because Brahms was irritable and gruff with adults. But he was a pussy cat with children; on the streets of Vienna he would dig into his large pockets and give candy to the children.

Menuhin: Well, that I didn't know. But that is my feeling about his music. He was a man who had all these great and good feelings, and probably was a man who was least able to express them outside his music.

Dubal: You may know the story, when Brahms left a party, he stood at the door and said, 'If there is anybody here tonight that I have not insulted, I apologize.' He was a terribly vulnerable man. He was capable of the finest friendships. His letters to Clara Schumann are treasures. There is one where he reports the last afternoon he spent with Schumann at the asylum which is touching and tragic.

Menuhin: There is a grandeur and nobility in his music, as well as mystery. I love his two serenades for orchestra, I've had such joy recently doing them. Whatever I know of Brahms, his trios, sonatas, quartets, concertos, there is always this north German mist. There are things happening behind shrouds. There is a great sense of mystery. Of course, there is also the good-natured boisterous Brahms who can show the common touch.

Dubal: He touched humanity at many points.

Menuhin: The integrity of Brahms was extraordinary: he burned anything that he felt was less than his best.

Dubal: You know that Arnold Schoenberg in 1947 wrote a marvellous piece titled 'Brahms the Progressive', almost fifty pages long, showing the many wonders of Brahms' mind, especially noting his asymmetrical structures.

Menuhin: I didn't know of that article – I must read it. Yes, for so long Brahms was considered an arch-conservative because in his day progressive music was 'the music of the future' of Liszt, Wagner and soon Richard Strauss.

Dubal: Which leads me to the colossus of that time, the most written about composer that ever lived –

Menuhin: Why yes, that must be Wagner – who portrayed

longing in the longest possible version. There is an unbroken
quality in his phraseology, which goes on and on into an
ecstatic infinity. I've done recently the *Siegfried Idyll*. It's a
piece that stretches itself. Do you know, the first piece I ever
conducted was the prelude to *Die Meistersinger*.

Dubal: So much music of the nineteenth century is frankly
erotic in nature – Mozart, or Bach, is not palpitating; Purcell,
and Palestrina, are chaste. But from Chopin, Liszt, Wagner,
through Debussy, music palpitates. So much of it is ecstatic
in nature. That is obviously what people want. Busoni once
wondered 'why the French had a persistent deafness to Berlioz
while putting Wagner, who is in every sense alien to them,
on a pedestal'. He said he was sure it was because 'Berlioz's
music is, above all, chaste. From 1830, most of music has
had to be erotic; whether *Tristan* or operetta. Wagner's music
is sexual, inactively erotic, thus *lascivious*. This also explains
why his inordinate duration is tolerated. Potency acts swiftly.
Eroticism is protracted.'

Menuhin: How very, very interesting. Many people have
thought how is it that people will sit through Wagner for so
long?

Dubal: I think Debussy said all those quarter-hour stretches
of boredom, for those wonderful minutes – I think it is akin
to the voyeur who will wait for hours for one good look – why
did this happen in art, not only in music, but poetry burns up
with love lyrics, and nineteenth-century painting is often
licentious. Was there a weakening in the fibre of society, or
had classicism become so sterile that the senses went riot?
Certainly all this spawned and paved the way to the sicken-
ing, crass, and commercial love songs. 'Baby, do you love
me?' –

Menuhin: Well, it was surely the beginning of the *rot*. But it
was none the less wonderful while it lasted. Because there

was a liberation of the human spirit. Just as in the sixties we experienced a post-war form of liberation. We could do what we wanted. It was a marvellous sensation for which we are paying a price now. But as long as it lasted it was marvellous. Society had been very structured before, and conventional. Not that the upper classes did not always allow themselves what they wanted. We have seen the development of indulgences which were once prohibited, or considered sinful by Jew, Christian, and Mohammedan. The democratic development caused this. Especially in the area of human passions, in which they were allowed to surface. And the development in music of harmony is of extreme importance here. Especially the sensuality of chromatic harmony. Music was mainly religious, except for the folk music, which was far more sensual than *musique savante*, a term which means music written down – structured and written down. Then came the admixture of the two. The folk influencing the *musique savante*. Already in the Bach suites, the gigues and sarabandes which had become stylized were originally folk. So that dance was the first element which intruded upon the *musique savante*, music used for the church. Then came the fact that religious music with the Protestant service enabled the congregation to take part in the singing, which before that was simply given to the congregation from above, the choir, or the priest chanting in the Gregorian chant. But it was very chaste, very monastic. Then came the mixture of the folk and singing from the congregation. The chorales that were sung are already less chaste than the Gregorian chants. Then came the Industrial Revolution, parliaments and personal expression.

Dubal: It then all moved very fast.

Menuhin: Yes, very fast. Romanticism became a sort of ego trip. My pain – my love, my suffering, a wonderful self-indulgence.

Dubal: On certain days, Yehudi – isn't *Tristan* repulsive? On certain days, it's a masterpiece, of course.

Menuhin: Yes, on certain days it is repulsive, on other days I still love and admire it. In the early twenties it was very attractive. Now when the bug of conducting gets under the skin I must say conducting the 'Liebestod' can be an extraordinary form of self-indulgence.

Dubal: Camus said, 'If I hear "La Vie en Rose" or the "Liebestod" once more, I'll collapse.'

Menuhin: I've certainly indulged myself. But you are perfectly right, it's simply something going a little too far. You can stretch and stretch and stretch only so much –

Dubal: The big composer for conductors today is Mahler –

Menuhin: I know – !

Dubal: In every Mahler work, you can hear the word itself – *Tristan – Tristan* lurking in the score. Mahler is repulsive – *I love him* – but he can nauseate me, my sensibility is insulted, I am manipulated.

Menuhin: Of course, he is a marvellous indulgence for conductors and big orchestras. You make a lot of noise, the music is on the whole easily understandable. Sometimes even trite, but highly emotional, and as you say palpitating – on the brink of heaven or hell. Of course, the new recruits to music like the Japanese or Chinese first fall in love with the Romantics. They can't resist it. They themselves have come out of very severely structured, restricted societies. All of a sudden they can scream at football and baseball. They can play romantic music and writhe with emotion. But the musicians are growing out of it now. They are producing wonderful musicians who play beautiful Bartók string quartets also.

Dubal: A composer who is surely well loved by you as a conductor is Handel. It's like a milk antidote after the Wagnerian and Mahlerian poisons.

Menuhin: Every time I come away from a recording session of Handel, I feel cleansed, it's wholesome music. These days there is so much music which is unwholesome; spending a day with this composer is always health-giving. He gives basically human emotion, clean, good, justifiable emotions – love, anger.

Dubal: A lusty human being – he reminds me of Boswell's personality.

Menuhin: Well, those were strong days. Men had to be strong, and they were strong because the whole upbringing including the diet was quite a strong one. And the air was clean. Handel had a power. He is a very great master.

Dubal: But Handel is almost unknown in his vast output. Today Bach is of course more prized. The English surely loved Handel. He is buried at Westminster Abbey, and the great oratorio tradition of England was spawned by him. Beethoven admired Handel and said, 'To him I bend the knee. Handel is the greatest and most capable composer that ever lived.'

Menuhin: But you are right, he is hardly played in proportion to his immense production. There are fashions that are dictated by what people are accustomed to, what they need. Their inclinations, and also their prejudices. All these elements enter the popularity of a given composer. Handel is far removed from our present day. It was a relatively simple age emotionally. I don't think they had these psychological conflicts of our time. We have fostered to a great degree inner conflicts. We are not certain of ourselves, not certain of values. We see so many different kinds of values, many that are thriving, and we often don't think they should thrive. It's sometimes difficult. I think that is not necessarily a loss. Somewhere in the individual there should be an inner balance. But then, to be buffeted between conflicting ideas is not a bad thing if you can reach some sort of resolution to the conflicts. That is important, otherwise everyone is left with one fanatical prejudice, whatever it might be. But a civilized society is one that no human situation can exist without an understanding of the polarities of the oppositions and can only be resolved by a dialogue and compromise. People often think that the human situation resembles the scientific one where you end up with one absolute fact. But the human situation is always in flux. But getting back to Handel, he was certainly played then much more freely than he is played today. His fast movements were played rather jazzy. Therefore some of the performances we have heard of Handel may not do it justice as would be required to enliven it, to make people really feel his impact. There were no metronomes, the style was freer. They obviously had a fine sense of rhythm. But it was an inner rhythm, it wasn't an outer rhythm, it didn't come from the metronome.

Dubal: Right. Rameau, born the same time as Handel, said, if one needed the rhythm indicated one wasn't musical –

Menuhin: Yes, exactly, yes, and we do, we have to have the legal document, so to speak. The composer has to say ninety-two to the quarter-note. And of course, we rarely reach the stage which we should, of forgetting it. We either never consult it, and may be off the mark, or having consulted it we often adhere to it too dogmatically. Handel's days were blissful days, those were the real romantic days, those were the days when young people fell in love with no idea of what they were in for. Neither family regulations nor number of children controlled, nor education decided upon. They were drawn into an irresistible relationship with their chosen one.

Dubal: What kind of city do you think Handel lived in, in the London he made such a hit in?

Menuhin: I think life then in London was very comfortable, and a very secure life. I imagine people were happy to flock to London; it must have offered a certain sense of reliability. In those days there must have been marvellous discussions. No telephones, they were person-to-person, and no recording instruments. We are constantly trying to analyse, re-analyse, compare, weigh the balance. I think it was a more spontaneous age.

Dubal: Elgar is also part of that Handel oratorio tradition.

Menuhin: Yes he is – but of course he is a devout romantic, and a part of him is influenced by the German. He went there, and it was the great conductor Hans Richter who first championed him. He is a composer of great warmth. Elgar is not overtly as sensual as say William Walton. But there is besides the German Straussian elements, a very real English-ness in his music. There is no bombast in his music, there is no hardness, there is no aggressiveness. I don't think the harmonic element ever becomes as dense as in Strauss. The meditative, musing quality of his slow movements have a touch of the folk melody of the English and the Irish.

Dubal: Your recording of the Elgar Concerto with the com-poser conducting is legendary. What type of conductor was he?

Menuhin: Elgar astonished me so much because he was so casual about it – casual about conducting and casual about the way he did it. He never tested me out. He heard me a few minutes. It was a summer's afternoon, a Saturday, I think, and then off to the races he went. And we met at the studios two days later, and he conducted that beautiful recording. A wonderful conductor, but again, without any of our frenzy, you know. In fact, it's true of his climaxes that they are benevolent climaxes. They should never be hard, they should never be played with sort of a Beethovenian sort of tragic attack. They are always, always gentle, even at their loudest.

Dubal: Let's say a few words about Vaughan Williams.

Menuhin: He is quintessentially English. He is deeply English. Deeply aware of his roots. In Vaughan Williams, there was the feeling of more than the folk tune. There is a composed eloquence, which recognized no barriers. There is wind, and water, and the colour green. The English landscape is infinite, there are so many varieties of green as far as the eye can see. When you look at the sea, it's sea as far as the eye can see, when you look at the sky, the same feeling occurs, and wind goes through everything. Therefore the elements are not broken up as in the Continental world, or the drier regions of the world where you have great rock faces, or in the mountainous regions where you have sheer cliffs and great differences in altitude, where you have violent contrasts. These violent contrasts are rather smoothed over in England, and that is perhaps why temperamentally they could evolve a civilization which is relatively tolerant – wars apart – and the music of Vaughan Williams has these long periods of just being carried by an atmosphere – a feeling. The contours of his music on the whole are smooth in move-ment. The great pastoral movements. Of course he wrote wonderful scherzi, sharp and witty. But for me Vaughan Williams is in those long movements where nothing much happens, but all is filled with English atmosphere.

Dubal: He looked like an aspect of England. He could have only been English. Did you know him at all?

Menuhin: Not well. I met him five or six times – a very self-sufficient, gentle human being, looking like a landslide. I'm

sure he was imbued with goodness – a thoroughly good man,
I think. (Vaughan Williams)

Dubal: The nine symphonies, I feel, are along with the Sibelius
and a few by Shostakovich amongst the great utterances of
post-Mahler symphonic form. You've conducted a great deal
of Vaughan Williams. How does this specifically English
master affect English audiences?

Menuhin: I think he evokes a very definite indigenous chord
when heard. Though England has changed a great deal since
Vaughan Williams, and in some respects this is a pity. With
the dissolution of the Empire a tradition died. It's always
the baby with the bath-water which is thrown out. The
Commonwealth was the largest assembly of like-minded
parliamentary, democratic nations in the world. It has
nothing to do with the United Nations. It has to do with
people that have shared a tradition. There is often an attempt
at downgrading the Commonwealth, as if it had no significance. So the reaction of Vaughan Williams is not the
same since the end of the war. England is Europeanized or
Americanized. They have our drinks, casinos, chains of
hotels, and so much more. The young looked up to the US
after the war, as the leader of the free world, and anything
American was sort of adopted. Others looked to Russia in
an entirely synthetic way for their ideals. On both counts,
they have lost that security of Englishness which was the
Englishman's calling card throughout the world. It was his
status – and glory. It mattered little if it was a naval officer or
composer or a shopkeeper. The knowledge of their Englishness gave them great security and strength.

Dubal: To be an Englishman almost was once a moral territory.
How fast things can change. As for adopting American ways,
the whole world does that. The United States with its materialism is quite simply the easiest recipe to imitate.

Menuhin: Yes, and this great sense of pride and tradition in England is fast vanishing. The English now feel we are nothing much on the face on the earth and other things are now more exciting. No, I doubt Vaughan Williams will have the same kind of audiences he once had; the part of his work which was really not exportable, the 'Englishness', will not be heard here any longer in the same way. The essence will be lessened, unfortunately.

Dubal: The Englishness will still be understood by the educated, but as a part of the nostalgia game. As we already hear in his orchestration of 'Greensleeves'. I want to also mention, for a bit, a master who is rapidly disappearing from the concert world, and who for me is also very English, Delius.

Menuhin: Delius is not easy to penetrate. Eric Fenby helped me very much with my own work on Delius. The Violin Concerto, the Double Concerto and the Violin Sonatas.

Dubal: Fenby's little book, *Delius as I Knew Him*, is one of the most intimate and honest little memoirs. A lovely little book.

Menuhin: Fenby is a very sensitive and gentle man. But he surely was tenacious. It must have taken incredible determination to bring those works to life from the paralysed Delius; it was an amazing act of reverence and dedication.

Dubal: And Delius was an impossible person!

Menuhin: Delius has an elusive, subtle, pastel quality. Somewhat impressionistic. He lived in France, and had many musical interests. We cannot treat him as purely English as we do Vaughan Williams. But it is not French music.

Dubal: Even the Violin Concerto could not have been composed by a so-called French Impressionist. Debussy would never have tolerated such amorphousness.

Menuhin: That's absolutely true! You put your finger on it. I'm a reflector, I bring no prejudice to music, I want to understand. I want to understand every phenomenon in the world, I want to understand every composer; and Delius came to me in its full impact through Fenby.

Dubal: Is it true you learned both concerti in four days? Glenn Gould called you a 'quick study'.

Menuhin: Oh, well, he was much more of a quick study than me.

Dubal: But four days, that sounds amazing. The Violin Concerto performance sounds so mellow.

Menuhin: Yes, four days, but I still used the music . . .

Dubal: Still, it sounds awesome to me. How do you account for only four days?

Menuhin: My only answer is I hate wasting time . . .

Dubal: I know you have personally known quite a few British composers. Have your retained your feeling for Walton's music?

Menuhin: Yes, indeed, I'm happy to say that I've just added the Sonata for string orchestra, which is his Quartet. It's one of the most brilliant works I've ever conducted. A work of *incredible* wit, originality, beauty, ranging from a scherzo which is as sharp and fast and stimulating as any scherzo you can imagine, to a slow movement of great contrast and profundity. Contrast between extreme quiet and great passion, a wonderful, wonderful work – I think certainly one of his great works.

Dubal: Well, he is a real romantic. You've done the Viola Concerto, and I believe the Violin Sonata is dedicated to you.

Menuhin: No, it's dedicated to Diana. I must tell you this

story. We were in Switzerland just after the war. The British
Council was doing a great deal to promote Benjamin Britten's
works, and they were doing his operas and other works.
Walton and a group of us were taking a walk. I remember
Walton needed Swiss francs. You were still then only allowed
to take five pounds out of Britain. I told Walton that I'd give
him some Swiss francs if he would compose a violin sonata
for me. I wanted him to take it seriously, because he took a
lot of time composing. So we walked to this music store,
which had this display in their shop window of Benjamin
Britten's music scores of his operas, his photograph and so
forth. And so we went in, and I bought him some music
papers to keep him to it. Diana and the others were outside of
the store, and all of a sudden they saw this big hand, which
was Walton's, come through the curtain of the store window
and taking hold of the picture of Ben Britten and turning it
face down.

Dubal: Oh, that's wonderful – perhaps a harmless little rivalry.
However, Walton's wife, Susana, wrote in her biography of
Walton that 'Throughout William's life, relations with other
composers were far from simple. When he spoke of Ben
Britten, he sometimes described him as his "junior partner";
William deplored and could not understand Ben surround-
ing himself with what he saw as a court of admirers and
hangers-on.'

Menuhin: Oh, well, it was still very English, it wasn't bitter at
all. Because Britten invited Walton to all his festivals.

Dubal: Who was your collaborator in the Walton Sonata?
Was it Kentner?

Menuhin: Yes, it was Louis Kentner, my brother-in-law.
And in fact the dedication is also to Griselda, Diana's sister,
Kentner's wife. We premiered it February 1950 at the Drury
Lane Theatre.

Dubal: There is another anecdote I would like to quote from Susana Walton's biography which is charming and so human. Mrs Walton said:

> Diana told me how William shocked her the day after her marriage. Yehudi was giving a recital in Leicester with the pianist Gerald Moore. As an encore, he had launched into the Bach D minor solo partita. William, who was there with Diana, said in a loud whisper, 'O God, not that Chaconne again! Come on, let's beat a retreat.' Diana, the embarrassed new bride, had had to say, 'No, William, you go if you want, but my place is here!'

Menuhin: Well, I suppose Bach didn't win the day for Walton.

Dubal: Have you played the Walton Viola Concerto much in public?

Menuhin: Oh, actually I only played the Concerto in public with him conducting in Birmingham and London. I was rather worried, but he wanted me to do it so much.

Dubal: I know how much you admired Benjamin Britten the musician, and loved him as a person. When did you first meet him?

Menuhin: At a party given by Mr Hawkes of Boosey and Hawkes, the publishers, just a week before I was going to go to Germany to play for the displaced persons at the camps. Ben desperately wanted to go along at all costs. Gerald Moore, the great accompanist, was coming with me, and indeed Ben came with us. Ben had a sensitivity beyond the normal. He was gentle and sensitive with the quality of an adolescent.

Dubal: What were some other of his primary personality characteristics?

Menuhin: Ben was an anxious person, terribly anxious about everything. Always wanted to win, if only for stability, if only for security. When we played cricket, Diana and he played on one side and Peter Pears and I on the other. At one point, Diana said to Ben, 'We *must* win this game, mustn't we?' And he said, 'Yes, Diana, how did you know?' Such a thing comes from a kind of inner insecurity or, putting it on a much higher level, the feverish need of a great creative mind to find satisfaction, to find security, to find achievement. He had this need to commune with people, especially with children. Very often with homosexuals or gays – they used to be called 'queers' – they have, at their best, a wonderful sensitivity for children, and Ben *adored* children. The works he wrote for children, *Noah's Ark* and other works, attest to this. He loved children's chorus. Of course, Ben wasn't married, but his long friendship with the tenor Peter Pears was an almost ideal marriage. Peter should have been a bishop; he had such great dignity. He inspired Britten's creativity and certainly helped to bring the literary element into Ben's life. He was a very young person. One had the feeling, with Ben, that one was in the presence of a tremendous creative genius who never grew up. And very fair.

Ben had this tireless avidity for life, for feeling and experiencing, and he was often excessive. Once, Diana was with Ben and Peter in Zurich and she told me they bought some chocolates and Ben ate himself silly with chocolates. He had to have his whisky before the concert and at the interval. And with it all, Ben, who was so kind, so touching, was also an elusive person, a sprite. Yes, you might call him a sprite! But above all he had a hunger for something great. He was always striving for it. And as you know, he was a wonderful pianist. Oh, the way he played Schubert songs, the *Winterreise* with Peter Pears, was unbelievable. The way he accompanied *me* – incomparable!

Dubal: There is great nostalgia for the Victorian age. In Britain the most important romantic composer before Elgar was William Sterndale Bennett (1819–68), but his expertly crafted music did not survive. It was too German – Mendelssohnian oriented – but what has survived from the Victorian English world, and still sounds healthy and hardy, are the theatre pieces of Gilbert and Sullivan.

Menuhin: I still am delighted with them. They fulfilled for a more innocent age what Irving Berlin, for example, did for Americans in his musicals. Gilbert and Sullivan are charming, full of wit, above all singable. You can dance to it, you leave the theatre feeling lighter.

Dubal: Do the English today still feel the security, the naïveté and delight of these Gilbert and Sullivan romps?

Menuhin: I doubt it, they have become too sophisticated – although they remain popular. Australia was the great place for Gilbert and Sullivan. Because they were still young and craving such musical entertainment: in fact it was in Australia that I heard my first Gilbert and Sullivan, and I was already nineteen years old.

Dubal: The giant presence in English serious music today is Tippett.

Menuhin: For the celebration of his eighty-fifth birthday, I'm conducting the work for double string orchestras. He is a musician of high ideals, a very quiet man. I've conducted also the Corelli variations. His music is very dense, harmonically; he is one of the densest English composers I know. I'm afraid I don't know his operas.

Dubal: Ah, there is so much music. I've always admired Gustav Holst, and I'm sorry that his superb *Planets* is over popular –

Menuhin: Holst I love, he has a real Englishness – and yes, it is a pity that the *Planets* have overwhelmed his large output. The choral works are excellent.

Dubal: Why do you think England during the eighteenth and nineteenth centuries did not produce great composers?

Menuhin: Being a very intuitive people, the English are not a philosophical people, they are not a mystical people. Surely they are a very musical people, especially the Scottish. Very musical, very romantic at heart. When you listen to the music of Purcell and Dowland, where the bar lines stand for nothing at all except a convenient reference, where the melody goes through bar lines, where the counterpoint criss-crosses, there is no fixed place of meeting at the bar line like with Schubert and Beethoven. The English could never easily accept the straight four-four and straight three-four of the Continent. I think that's one reason, and that in a freer age, when composition became freer in the late nineteenth century, the English re-established their links with their past, with Dowland, Purcell and the Elizabethans.

Dubal: A composer whose status today is far less than even half a century ago is Gluck. Haydn, Mozart and Beethoven grew up on him, Berlioz and Wagner adored him. Do you have any thoughts on him?

Menuhin: He was considered one of music's immortals, and his operas have become relegated to a limbo. I too only know *Orfeo*, but when I first heard it [hums] it was a big moment for me. I was then ten or eleven and deeply affected by it.

Dubal: A composer much performed but still undervalued is Haydn, who has been compared too much to his friend Mozart, and is so much different than the Salzburg Master.

Menuhin: I love Haydn dearly – I think he is one of the very great composers. I've done more and more Haydn. Haydn has no inhibitions, he will come up with the most extraordinary surprises. Of course, he was so prolific, not all of his works are of the highest. The great 'Salomon' or 'London' symphonies are the high point of his symphonic career.

Dubal: Yes, for me this series is the glorious manifestation of his work, where his ever-expanding mind created within the 'sonata idea' one of the great bodies of abstract music. If Beethoven had never lived, the 'London' symphonies would be perceived as one of Western culture's great intellectual achievements.

Menuhin: Yes, but Beethoven then overshadows him, and Haydn became relegated as a precursor of the Beethoven symphonies. What always strikes me about Haydn, as it does of Handel, is their overwhelming devoutness. They wrote for the glory of God. Haydn was a happy, balanced and fulfilled man. He could write music out of a secure sense of right and wrong, and human dignity.

Dubal: You know that more Mendelssohn is coming back to the living repertoire.

Menuhin: Yes he is. He lived too short a life, but was incredibly gifted. His symphonies are quite wonderful. He is the lucid romantic. But people are never grateful for happiness, and Mendelssohn is so often radiantly happy –

Dubal: Felix means 'happy' in Latin.

Menuhin: But people grow tired of being happy. They want drama, adventure, danger and aggression. When they meet someone who writes so perfectly, so sunnily, they grow weary of it. It's a little like Switzerland. People tire of Switzerland: it's too well run, everything is in perfect order. I must say I'm only grateful for such things – I'm not one who needs to escape to Nicaragua. We need to keep a place in our hearts for the Mendelssohns.

Dubal: He had everything from wealth and breeding to the

28

highest talent, and his sunny nature gave the world a new form
of romanticism – the *scherzando*, Oberon world – as well as a
picturesque romanticism which is his true contribution: so
different from the Chopinesque *morbidezza* or the Wagnerian
eroticism, or the Schumannian madness –

Menuhin: Imagine composing the octet at fifteen, the
overture to the *Midsummer Night's Dream* at seventeen – are
these not miracles? He also was a wonderful letter writer,
and drew and painted in watercolours beautifully. He was a
remarkable pianist and conductor. All this, and he died at
thirty-eight.

Dubal: We cannot even estimate the greatness of Schubert –
and he died at thirty-one.

Menuhin: And Schubert came at a time when only he could
have come, and only in Vienna. He is the true product of that
city. Mozart, Haydn, Beethoven, they were transplanted
there. 'Schubert belongs to that fresh, tender time, those
running brooks,' he is the idealization of the period. He
is tender youth, the bud, the seed, those tender feelings.
Schubert felt the intensity of young feeling. There is that
feeling of youth, adolescence and a sense of death. One feels
he could gamble away life for one emotion, one sensation –
the sacrifice of youthful love, for instance. Schubert's music
has an intensity that has not been grabbed by practical life
which channels and reduces that intensity. In his music these
heightened emotions are channelled into a purity, without
objects. It's purity itself.

Dubal: Schubert is surely one of the most complex interpre-
tively of all composers. The psychological elements cannot
be described.

Menuhin: I can never listen to the *Winterreise* without tears.
That sense of total giving, of love, sacrifice and passion, a

sense of ecstatic sacrifice. It doesn't know what it is for. But it seizes one, and when we listen to the music of Schubert, I think that everyone relives those moments. Those moments on the verge, so to speak, which of course no words can describe.

Dubal: Perhaps that's what Schumann meant when he called Schubert's music 'everlasting youth'.

Menuhin: Yes, it was also a Vienna of woods and pure air – it was still a feudal world. The Industrial Revolution had not made its impact there as, for instance, in London. There were great creative powers as well as emotional security in the Vienna of Schubert's time.

Dubal: Let's speak a moment of one of Schubert's first critical sponsors, who discovered the manuscripts of Schubert's great Ninth Symphony, and sent it to Mendelssohn to conduct. Of course I'm talking about that troubled and so human Schumann.

Menuhin: As you say, troubled – a genius, no question – he was tormented, and what toil and effort he must have gone through to put down those ideas. His music is very problematic. Many an interpreter has been defeated by his enigmatic world.

Dubal: I think he was the most romantic composer of them all – and the interpreter must be creative to bring him off because of his problematic element. Your record of the D minor Sonata with Hephzibah is wonderful.

Menuhin: I came to that work through Enesco, who loved it. Benjamin Britten loved Schumann. In Schumann you have to give him shape, you must clarify, he can be awfully thick. I remember working so well together with my sister on the D minor Sonata.

Dubal: Throughout your life you have sung the praises of Enesco, perhaps the supreme musical influence of your life . . .

Menuhin: He was unique and unapproachable as a musician. It was Enesco who opened my musical mind, so to speak. I was around eleven, and he had me hear Balinese music, and recordings of African music. It was really this small step which led me to try to expand my musical world into musics other than my classical training. From here I would be able to enter the world of Ravi Shankar, a divine musician, a dear person. Indian music opened a fresh reservoir for me. As did my experience with Grappelli and jazz and improvisation.

As a young boy I revelled in the Enesco Third Violin Sonata composed in the manner of the Rumanian popular style. In this work I feel closer to the gypsy violinist. But my training had probably been too rigid to ever improvise the way I dreamed. But in this sonata, with its marvellous content, I at least could impersonate the gypsy violinist, as if I was given a text and playing a role. The work is a masterpiece of notation, and Enesco put every nuance, every shade of gypsy style into this particular work. You know, Enesco had an unerring sense of style, but the feeling of living, breathing improvisation was part of his playing even when playing a standard work by Bach or Brahms. This sense of the interpreter composing the work at the moment, is one of the rarest interpretive abilities.

Dubal: Yes, you mention his notation, of which he is a meticulous master. The score for example of his Third Piano Sonata is notated with such precision; Lipatti's recording of it is a marvel.

Menuhin: Enesco was Lipatti's godfather. Unfortunately Enesco's very real genius as a composer has never been given its due. He evolved an idiom all his own in opera, songs and chamber music, as well as symphonies. His harmonic sense was fastidious.

Dubal: Let's hope, in his case, musicians and the public go beyond his celebrated *Rumanian Rhapsody*.

Menuhin: Exactly, I hope so. It has not been easy for his music to make its way, as Bartók's did. Enesco was a delicate mixture of elements which could have happened only in Vienna, where he studied. The folk and gypsy roots of Rumania and Hungary blended with the high cultivation of Western Europe, which gave Vienna an incredible musical wealth. Enesco the man was a true aristocrat, polished, educated, refined, and a musician the likes of whom I have never seen equalled, with a musical memory that cannot be described.

Dubal: You have said to me that you are a pygmy compared to Enesco. Are you just being modest?

Menuhin: Please believe me, David, that I'm very serious. I've just mentioned his musical memory. Mine can't compare, nor do I have a gift for composition, nor his skills as a pianist. I am much less in sheer talent, and the repertoire he knew by heart . . .! I will never know anything close to his knowledge of music.

Dubal: Someone once thought he was sight-reading and mentioned what a great facility he had. Enesco replied, 'I'm not sight-reading. I know everything.'

Menuhin: Of course, he could sight-read also enormously well – and I must mention his intellectual gifts, and the depth of his soul. His spiritual qualities were above all others.

Dubal: Do you think at least you ever played the violin as well as Enesco?

Menuhin: Absolutely not – I could never match his playing. However, thankfully his spirit and his teaching dwell in me –

I know this, of course, in certain aspects of how I play and interpret and analyse scores. I also feel his presence in certain attitudes to life and to people. Enesco was extremely chivalrous, and this appealed to the romantic aspects of my nature.

Dubal: And how did he teach you?

Menuhin: He could tell me something which would ignite me. After all, ignition is the supreme quality in teaching. For example, he wrote on my violin part of the Beethoven Concerto, before the second big tutti where the violin plays loftily and rises ever higher, here Enesco wrote simply 'contained dignity'. He didn't use many words at lessons. You see, he would sit at the piano and accompany me, and his playing was so pure and deep that he spoke to me through the music.

Dubal: Did he teach you the Elgar Concerto?

Menuhin: In the second subject of the first movement of the Elgar, Enesco said, 'Oh, that is very English!' At that time I didn't know exactly what that meant. But Enesco was speaking of a kind of quality of adult innocence. It is something earthy, and sublime – and it's in the music, deep inside and yet very apparent. Enesco had a grasp, an uncanny instinct, about various peoples, and nations. My family used French or Italian ships when crossing the Atlantic. But Enesco said, 'I travel on English boats, the British know more about the sea than anyone else.' Even though Enesco spent little time in England, he understood perfectly the country and its people.

Dubal: I know that you are fond of Ernest Bloch's music. Since his death, his music has suffered an eclipse. He seems hard to put in a category.

Menuhin: Very hard for the people who like to pigeonhole,

also Bloch's rhapsodic style is hard to formulate, since his music is very largely a series of statements and meditations, although he is the most famous Swiss composer, and he always returned there, and loved the mountains. Bloch is essentially a Jewish composer, in his deep and guttural feeling for the Jewish cry of despair.

Dubal: I think his art is deeply penetrating. The string quartets are an extraordinary contribution to the form. There is a burning passion, also a frustration, as well as a sarcastic irony at times.

Menuhin: I fully agree, and he was tortured – a prophetic man who looked astonishingly like an Old Testament face. He wrote beautifully for the violin – you know he was a very good player. Do you know that the first piece I ever played by a living composer was by Bloch, a wonderful piece called *Avodah* which he composed for me. I was a child of about seven or eight. Bloch was a great teacher. And he was the director of the San Francisco Conservatory.

Dubal: Do you have any thoughts about Fauré?

Menuhin: He is one of those composers who kept developing throughout his career. He is an important composer. He evolved much like Beethoven in the spiritual sense.

Dubal: Yes, who would have guessed that the Fauré of the early works such as the Ballade for piano and orchestra or the First Violin Sonata, would have composed the String Quartet, a work that like Beethoven was composed by Fauré in the state of being deaf.

Menuhin: Yes, exactly so, the early music may be more charming, but the depth of the late music grows upon many hearings. I, of course, played the First Sonata, and Benjamin Britten, who loved Fauré, wanted me to do the late Second Sonata, which indeed we did do together, but unfortunately it wasn't recorded. It is a reflective and interesting work. I wish I knew more of the modern French masters such as Messiaen, who is so much admired, and Boulez, who is such a brilliant musical mind. His *Marteau Sans Maître* is interesting and he is a superb conductor. He aims for and gets the most extraordinary clarity. In Berg and Stravinsky, he is fantastic.

Dubal: Did you perform any Ravel?

Menuhin: I played the trio, I played the *Tzigane* a great deal. Nobody played it better than Enesco, who introduced me to Ravel. The *Tzigane* is a piece that is torn apart in performance. Enesco wasn't a gypsy by blood, but how he understood the gypsy element. The Violin Sonata has a blues movement. Ravel's grasp of various styles is amazing.

Dubal: What of Berlioz?

Menuhin: Oh, he is marvellous. Such originality and audacity. I loved conducting the *Symphonie Fantastique*. It doesn't seem to age. It was entirely new.

Dubal: It glows, the orchestra suddenly becomes a pliable instrument in his orchestration. It's amazing the change in sentiment in the *Symphonie Fantastique*, as compared with the Viennese classical school. The Romantic neurotic sensibility is already full-blown, and it was only composed three or four years after Beethoven's death.

Menuhin: Yes, it is amazing. Berlioz was a literary man, and anything and everything stimulated him. I've done *Harold in Italy*, the viola part – and this work was inspired by Byron, who was the arch-Romantic who inspired so much Romantic music –

Dubal: I know how you have yearned to conduct *Carmen*.

Menuhin: I hope still to do it. What an overwhelming talent

35

Bizet was. I love that symphony Beecham used to do. I've conducted it also. What a charming work.

Dubal: Yes, the Symphony in C, a gem. Balanchine made a beautiful ballet to it. Bizet composed it at seventeen, imagine such precocity. He died so early – I believe at thirty-eight. *Carmen* is the world's most performed opera. Why does it have this universal appeal? Nietzsche loved it, Tchaikovsky loved it, and people that generally don't like opera love it.

Menuhin: I just adore *Carmen* – it appeals to the nomad and gypsy in our heart. It has sacrifice, high drama, fate and death. The mad disregard for any convention, the disregard for any barriers whatsoever. There is a tragic love. I cannot compare it to any other opera, my love for *Carmen* is in a separate category.

Dubal: Well, she was quite a *femme fatale.* Do you love Debussy?

Menuhin: Deeply. Like the Impressionist painters, he brought to music something totally new. It has nothing to do with reality and yet everything to do with a subjective reality. Debussy probes what is really inside us, and he is always unpredictable. From one part to the next, you never know what will happen.

Dubal: He is truly one of music's original beings. The pianist Claudio Arrau told me he thought it was music from another planet.

Menuhin: Yes, the mature music of Debussy must have, in its own time especially, sounded like a new musical art-form.

Dubal: He took up Liszt's mantle and began breaking the Germanic stranglehold on music. Debussy even de-Europeanized music, weaving the pentatonic and whole tone scales into a very sensuous and oriental art.

Menuhin: Wagner extended and Debussy condensed. The piano preludes, for instance, are no more than two or two and a half minutes long in most cases. That's also very French, this reducing element, but Debussy did it all with new sensations. Even in their food, the French condense; they boil down.

Dubal: Do you think that the French really have a great love for music?

Menuhin: The French have an intellectual passion for every art. The French are capable of love, but they are so sophisticated; their love must always be within a mixture of love and intellectual content. The Germans can love indiscriminately. The French love is never indiscriminate. Nor is it ever free of a critical faculty. The French aren't really a musical nation, but their musical public is one of the best in the world because there's nothing they do or that they cultivate that isn't cultivated with the mind. So they will know if you're playing in style or not. They won't say, 'Oh, I love him, he has the most beautiful sound.' No, no. You'll have to have more than that to please them.

Dubal: Do you have special feelings about Debussy's late Violin Sonata?

Menuhin: That work has been growing on me more than any other composition. I can never get deep enough into it. It's a masterwork. It's a masterpiece of the unpredictable, but with a logic that goes through the unpredictable, that is what fascinates me in it. It's a study of fate in miniature, always bringing the unpredictable event, and yet it makes total sense.

Dubal: Do you consider yourself to be a curator and caretaker of the masterpieces that you now play?

Menuhin: Exactly. Or even of the violin that I supposedly

own. I hope I can pass it on. In fact, if it was stolen, I'd much rather it was stolen by someone who loved it and could play it.

Dubal: Which is the greatest of the modern violin concertos?

Menuhin: The Bartók, I would say. Oh, yes!

Dubal: What an occasion in your life it must have been when you opened up that package which contained Bartók's solo sonata written for you.

Menuhin: But my heart fell. I thought I could never play the work. And yet I knew I was going to play it, and I *did* play it within a month. Fortunately, I did play it and he could hear it.

Dubal: Within a month!

Menuhin: Yes, I did. I played it from memory. He came to the concert and he was pleased. Although I know that he must have listened for what he knew it would become. Bartók was one of the greatest men I ever met.

Dubal: What a wonderfully sensitive face.

Menuhin: Yes, a wonderfully sensitive face. But he was already sick, already had leukaemia at the time I knew him. He was going, you know, to do two things had he lived another few years. He had accepted a teaching post at Northwestern University in Seattle, to spend two years with the Red Indians of the Northwest. They would have gained a musical language of their own. I often say that every culture should have its own Bartók. And he was going to spend a summer, what would have been the summer of '43, with me in California. That never happened, to my endless regret. He couldn't come out because of his physical condition. Imagine what I would have learned being with Bartók for a summer.

Dubal: Supposedly he knew so much of many things.

Menuhin: He was an incredibly erudite man. Not only about music or languages but also botany, and whatever he touched in life or whatever drew his attention, he studied. And I'm sure if you asked him about the anatomy of a horse, he could tell you about it in depth, or why plants grew on certain sides of a river, and the soil, the climate, the humidity, whatever it was. He was one of these born scholars – *and yet a creator*. That was his greatness, that he combined the methodical with the creative. There are few people like that; some people are creative without being methodical, and others are methodical with no touch of creation. He could order those thousands of melodies he had collected in his wanderings. The work of a real scholar.

Dubal: What do you think Schoenberg meant when he said that he feared his music may be too ugly?

Menuhin: I didn't realize he said that. How very interesting. It means that he wasn't one with his music.

Dubal: He was a man who wasn't one with many things.

Menuhin: So he was writing things that weren't necessarily out of his aesthetic convictions.

Dubal: Perhaps that's true. Because he came out of the Wagnerian world, and his first works are saturated with hyper-chromaticism. You know, he literally gave up his music for about three years after *Pierrot Lunaire* and devoted himself to painting.

Menuhin: I didn't know that.

Dubal: Then began his years with the twelve-tone method. Perhaps he wasn't one with this method, but he knew he couldn't continue living under the power of Wagnerism. That had to be over with. And certainly, many composers felt this.

Menuhin: I didn't know about his paintings.

Dubal: They are excellent. His self-portraits and his portrait of Alban Berg are wonderful. There was a major exhibit in New York of his paintings which showed him to be equal to some of the minor German Expressionists of his time. Schoenberg insisted that he was an amateur at painting, but, then again, he was also self-taught as a composer. And he didn't differentiate, he said, between his creation of music and painting.

You were not really in sympathy with Schoenberg's music, yet you did play Schoenberg's Fantasy for violin and piano.

Menuhin: Yes, I've always gone to the source, so to speak, and I would not have learnt it without Glenn Gould, who for me was the source for that piece. I couldn't have played it with anybody else. Glenn was an authority and loved it. I always feel somehow that people who love somebody or something or some work are nearer the truth than the ones who hate it. So if I want to know a new work, it's nice to get to know the work through someone who sees the best in it. The same thing happened with the Berg Concerto. It was Ansermet who said, 'You must play the Berg Concerto.' Well, of course, nobody knew it better than Ansermet. And when I did it for the first time, it was with him. Although Ansermet loved the concerto, I had reservations about it. I was absolutely surprised when people came backstage, because I wasn't moved.

Dubal: But are you now?

Menuhin: A little more. But it moved others, which irritated me. I was irritated by myself. I was playing something that moved others but didn't move me.

Dubal: Why do you think the vast amount of music written in Schoenberg's twelve-tone system has not survived?

Menuhin: I think it is an arbitrary system, there's no gainsaying that. Because every note is supposed to be equal, and notes are no more equal than human beings are equal.

Dubal: Perhaps here lies an aesthetic fallacy.

Menuhin: I think so. And yet such is the genius and gift of great composers such as Schoenberg and Webern that they can constrain themselves to any system and produce great music.

Dubal: Let's speak a bit on a few Russian composers. Prokofiev has held his own in the ocean of twentieth-century music.

Menuhin: I admire Prokofiev. The sharp edge of his wit is devastating, and the smoothness of his transitions. And there is the tongue in cheek of so much of his music. In some ways, Prokofiev and Stravinsky have much in common. They both have a high degree of Russian quality as well as a precision which is like a scalpel, and they have the same intellectual curiosity. Some of their music has the precision of a metallic instrument which cuts with a perfect edge. Both composers have exceptionally clear minds, as well as a feeling for the grandiose in spite of their precision.

Dubal: Prokofiev and Stravinsky share a wonderful ironic streak. But Prokofiev possesses a true romantic lyricism which Stravinsky basically lacks. Poulenc called Prokofiev the Russian Liszt.

Menuhin: I didn't know that. How interesting. Certainly Prokofiev has music of high interest in every form. The violin and piano concerti are repertory pieces, the symphonies are full of variety and the ballets are true descendants of Tchaikovsky.

Dubal: Well, Tchaikovsky's ballets are incomparable works

of dance. I think it was Nureyev who said every ballet dancer, each morning, should bow in front of Tchaikovsky's portrait.

Menuhin: Tchaikovsky remains a giant. He just simply wrote and wrote spontaneously. He touched the human heart. I feel his music is largely balletic.

Dubal: Yes, Taneyev criticized Tchaikovsky for that balletic quality even in such a symphonic work as the Fourth Symphony.

Menuhin: I don't think of it as a criticism. I think it's a criticism of many of his interpreters, who allow the weight to crush the elegance. I feel Tchaikovsky is a very elegant and aristocratic composer.

Dubal: Yes, I totally agree. He is often played with such turbulence and hysteria that the natural suavity and innocence of much of his music is forsaken. Conductors so often use the symphonies as merely colourful vehicles, and pianists and violinists use the concerti as examples of the 'wow technique'. What is also forgotten is that Tchaikovsky had a fine sense of form, and of his contemporaries only Brahms is his superior in structural matters.

Menuhin: I quite agree. People refuse to give him his due on many levels, and certainly they lose touch with his elegance.

Dubal: He was one of the few Russians of his time who worshipped Mozart. There is a touching letter where he practically begs his patroness Madame von Meck to change her mind about Mozart. 'How can you not love Mozart?' he beseeched her.

Menuhin: What a wonderful heart he had. In conducting his greatest and most powerful works, one must remember his inherent elegance, as well as the dance-like qualities. I love

dearly the Fourth, Fifth and Sixth Symphonies. When I
was a child, an innocent child, my favourite piece was the
Sérénade Mélancolique. The Violin Concerto I played so
much when very young. I felt that I never brought to it
something unique. I loved the performances of Heifetz and
Oistrakh.

Dubal: Did you know Shostakovich?

Menuhin: I met him when I went back to Moscow in 1945. I
saw him many times in Prague, in London and in New York.
He always seemed a sad figure, very sad. He was so shy, and
he looked like a very frightened man. When you read and
hear his music you cannot believe that it was composed by
someone so shy and frightened looking. But obviously it
belied an inner power and conviction. In fact, the outer
fright drove the power inside which then came out in music.
These dichotomies and paradoxes in human beings are so
inscrutable. We can know the real Shostakovich not through
the person, but through his art. I also feel we cannot know a
people, a nation, until we know their music.

Dubal: Do you know much of Rimsky-Korsakov's work,
which is not known in the West as much as it should be?

Menuhin: I'd love to see his operas, which so fascinated his
own time. I feel attracted to what I know of his work.

Dubal: Yes, those that know Rimsky are often crazy about
him. Stravinsky studied with him. Horowitz would often
play for me transcriptions he made from his operas, that he
never played publicly; and Rachmaninoff, who conducted
many of Rimsky's operas, was absolutely in love with them.

Menuhin: Yes, how really extraordinary, and how lucky to
have heard those Horowitz transcriptions.

Dubal: Bernstein's death has been mourned worldwide –

he was undoubtedly a genius. I think his music will wear well in the future.

Menuhin: He will be missed terribly. I think *On the Town* is marvellous and brilliant. The musical *West Side Story* is now known to everybody. He is the real son of New York. There is no one more characteristically New York than Bernstein, in its best, most cosmopolitan sense. He is a musician deeply engaged. Whatever he touches is with such intensity, such conviction. It applies to his conducting, to his composing. Even to his piano playing.

Dubal: Oh yes, what a *Rhapsody in Blue* he plays. Yet this child of New York is the most eclectic musician of all. His conducting of the Nielsen symphonies is the finest ever, his Mahler has been taken for supreme. Ives, Copland, Haydn, Beethoven are all equal food for his musical tastes.

Menuhin: That is the finest example of New York. That is why I link Lenny and New York together. New York is the place where all these styles, tendencies and peoples have come. There is no city that is as much a part of the whole.

Dubal: Do you know anything of Aaron Copland's music, which I admire?

Menuhin: I'm very fond of Copland, and I know him quite well. I once did an interview with him.

Dubal: I knew him well, we did a year-long radio series together. What a fine man.

Menuhin: Oh yes, very fine. Very American. Jewish, like Lenny. Being New Yorkers, they are very American.

Dubal: Yes, the amazing adaptability of the Jew. Nobody could write of the prairie or the Wild West, or the Appalachian Mountains, better than this Jew born in Brooklyn.

Menuhin: Yes, this understanding and analytic quality was characteristic of many Jews of Copland's period who were grafted into the American melting pot.

Dubal: We must speak of Gershwin. Have you ever conducted anything by him?

Menuhin: Yes, only recently – *An American in Paris*. You know, I had never conducted Gershwin before. He was certainly a genius. I met him in New York when I was a boy.

Dubal: What year was this?

Menuhin: Around 1930 or '31, which means he was thirty-two and already famous. He arrived at a house of our mutual acquaintance. After saying a few words, he stalked to the piano, this gaunt man, and began to play. He didn't want to talk, he wanted to play. He was one of those who burnt himself out creating. The piano was a compulsion to him, talking was merely an amenity. He was not interested in anything but transforming life into a musical language.

Dubal: Gershwin died at thirty-eight. *An American in Paris*, the Piano Concerto, *Rhapsody in Blue* and a few others are his only concert pieces. How do you rank them?

Menuhin: His weaknesses are evident in all his large concert pieces. The structural seams can show. But give me these pieces anytime over any merely beautifully structured piece. Gershwin has drive, imagination, rhythmic twists and all the patterns that became the code of jazz. But in a sense, it was only when conducting *An American in Paris* that I really felt Gershwin's strength. In fact, while conducting the piece, I *knew* I was born in New York. The work is cutting, ironic, sarcastic, elegant and with a real New York wit.

Dubal: Let's mention some of those precursors of modern violin composition, that wonderful group of Italian violin composers of the eighteenth century – the pre-Paganini stars.

Menuhin: Oh yes, what a choir of stars: Vivaldi, Corelli, Tartini, Locatelli, Vitali, Viotti – they are amazing. They loved the violin, of course they loved the voice – in the violin they had a craving for beautiful sound. I'm convinced that all these violinists used vibrato. I'm not going to accept that they didn't know or use vibrato – they couldn't be Italian, they couldn't love singing, the human voice. Nor is a vibrato an alien thing. You can't deliberately separate it from violin playing, certainly not if you are a natural violinist.

Dubal: I know you have also enjoyed conducting the concerti grossi of these violin composers, such as the Corelli concerti grossi. They are filled with verve.

Menuhin: I love them. In Berlin, I recently did the Christmas Concerto of Corelli. What is curious about all that music of Vivaldi and Corelli is it looks deceptively simple, and yet it has an organic structure which is very closely knit. As soon as one begins studying a few bars, one finds an incredible complexity in terms of counterpoint, fugal elements, bass line, imitation, and other compositional devices.

Dubal: I wish more Locatelli was played – he had a very special understanding of the violin.

Menuhin: Oh, a real virtuoso. Locatelli's concerti are very, very difficult. It's a great shame that they are not played.

Dubal: What is Leopold Mozart's position in the history of your instrument?

Menuhin: Well, he left one of the best violin manuals, guides. Not only through the technique, but even to the interpretation of ornaments – grace notes and that kind of thing – very valuable. Obviously, an extremely experienced and good musician, there's no question of that. I'm sure Leopold was essential to his son; I don't think his son would have progressed, would have been the child genius he was, without his father.

Dubal: Leopold gets a bad press these days because of the play *Amadeus*.

Menuhin: Yes. Diana saw the play, I saw the film in Bonn. I must say, however distorting it may be of some historical accuracies, I found it rather moving.

Dubal: Yes, and good theatre. But many people don't want their heroes caricatured, or made to seem ridiculous.

Menuhin: So true! Schaffer wrote an excellent article that appeared in the London *Times*. I felt strongly about what he said about Mozart's opera *La Clemenza di Tito*, which is all in major and yet encompasses every possible depth of emotion in tragedy. The Russian Jew, for instance, can't imagine such a thing. It must be in minor to be tragic. Yet Mozart in the framework of perfect courtly courtesy, of the gentle, of the polite, never offending, never shocking, and yet he conveys the most intense passions *and* in the major mode. And if you look at the score, just as with Beethoven, you would say, 'Well, that's a series of scales and arpeggii in G major or D major.' In Mozart you say, 'These are conventional turns of phrase.' You just have to go a little deeper into them, and then you realize suddenly the magic is quite unbelievable.

Dubal: Have you thought why the violin has captured the imagination of so many types of music lovers from the concert hall to the square dance?

Menuhin: There is certainly a great attraction that the violinist exercises on the audiences. For one thing, the sound evoked is very near to the human voice and the throbbing of vibrato.

The violin and the bow as well become a kind of extended limb, and there is a mysterious quality about this sound coming from an instrument.

The violin conveys emotion as I think nothing other than the human voice can. But the human voice somehow doesn't always look beautiful. The open mouth, the gaping mouth, isn't always beautiful, whereas the violinist seems in a certain way to be a ventriloquist in that it seems to come from something within him that isn't himself. It's more than himself and it's secret, and that quality seems to evoke something from an audience that no other instrument does.

Dubal: What is most inimitable about a violinist's musical personality?

Menuhin: Oh, the sound of the violinist – it's as personal as the sound of a singer. Heifetz's sound was unique, Elman's, Oistrakh, Kreisler, Enesco's still rings in my ear. For a long time critics who talked about phrasing and structure, and so on and on, seldom mentioned the tone quality of the violinist. Finally it's being talked about again. The describing of a specific violinist's sound is important for critics to attempt, at least.

Dubal: James Huneker said that of all the instruments the violin has the most delicate nervous system.

Menuhin: I think that is true – much more delicate than the viola, for instance. The proof of it is that there are quite a few very fine modern viola makers. But they haven't yet made a really great viola to compare with the great Italians of the past. The violin is indeed the most delicate of instruments, and it speaks to people in a way that is deeply human.

Dubal: There is a magnetism that a violinist can possess that perhaps no other instrumentalist has on stage. Paganini himself said, 'I am as ugly as sin, yet all I have to do is play my violin and women fall at my feet.' Also the violin soloist has a freedom on stage that is unique.

Menuhin: Exactly. He can move on his feet. The pianist is tethered to his instrument, which in itself is a rather clumsy-looking affair. I have teased my son Jeremy every time I can find some new use for the piano which is not musical. Oh, recently, I heard a new use for the piano. One of my friends visited the Steinways in their summer house. There was a lake there, and they were taken to a little rowboat which looked charming, which was in fact made from Steinway grand pianos. And so I said, 'Well, there at least is a practical use for the piano.' But of course I love the piano.

Dubal: Would you say the sound and shape of the violin is in the collective unconscious?

Menuhin: Very much so. There is hardly a country, a culture, that doesn't have its stringed, bowed instrument. If you ever have a chance to visit the Folk Instrumental Museum in Moscow, to see the variety of violins, village violins made by the carpenters, the craftsmen of those villages, it's unbelievable. We think of a violin in its glorious crystallized form as it finally evolved in Italy – in Cremona and elsewhere in Italy – in the seventeenth century. But when you see the efforts at making string bowed instruments in the little villages and the music that must have been played on them – dance music, engaging, entertaining, tuneful music – and then think of the gypsies who also didn't have ready-made fiddles, you begin to understand what the background of the violin is and why I have always felt that improvisation, and the playing of the violin by ear, is the most important aspect of learning to play the violin. It's the improvisatory quality of the violinist that he brings to the instrument which is, I think, the essence of violin playing.

Dubal: How do you think the violin evolved?

Menuhin: The first vibrating string was probably the string of a bow and arrow. A string that held two ends of a bent stick at tension and made a certain sound. And that the first sound of a stringed instrument would be two bows, as it were, drawn at right angles to each other. Either it evolved simultaneously as a musical instrument and as the instrument of the hunt, or of the amorous instrument, the arrow through the heart, Diana. It may have evolved simultaneously, just as I am absolutely convinced that music came before language. Because music is organized sound, pure sound, organized noise perhaps first, but then sound and rhythm, and that must have preceded language and the alphabet. There can be no question but that man sang before, or made at least the noise of singing and calling before he put syllables to it. Whether the first musical instrument, stringed musical instrument, was used as a weapon or a musical instrument, that probably will never be known. But I think man in his early curiosity must have attached a string to a twig and bent it for some reason or other, and then found that it vibrated.

Dubal: Did you ever feel trapped or repelled by the violin in your life?

Menuhin: At times I felt I wasn't worthy of what I was trying to capture or express on the violin. But those periods always passed with a new discovery, and a new ability. I emerged to simply live with that. Of course, sometimes at my very best I wish I could have re-recorded everything I've ever done.

Dubal: The violin is so delicate. When you conduct, you are working with the largest instrument.

Menuhin: It's the contrast I like. The violin is in millimetres – you need to be precise about pressures and pitch. It's a mar- vellous discipline. It's like walking a tight-rope. My day isn't really a day for me unless I have practised. Without it, something is missing. It's a lifetime habit. Conducting is larger than life; it's great fun, but it's a great responsibility.

Dubal: Your face has become in the world psyche the way a violinist should look. That at least has been my feeling since I was twelve years old or so.

Menuhin: But how can you say that, when actually the most famous and most characteristic violinist's face is Paganini's? *That* was considered how a violinist should look, something devilish about him, something irresistibly evil, perhaps, and inspired.

Dubal: Well, I feel you should have had the part of Paganini instead of Stewart Granger in *The Magic Bow*, the film on Paganini.

Menuhin: Oh, if you had seen my acting capacity, it is nil! I can't act. But I did encourage them to give me a film test because that was their idea, too. It was the time I was courting Diana in London, in 1945. I was amused to have a film test. It seemed the only opportunity I might ever have, although I knew perfectly well that I didn't have the time, even if I had had the talent. But I led them on that way. So I was dutifully dressed in those shoes with silver buckles and breeches and the elegant lace shirts, to look as near as possible to how Paganini may have looked. Then I had to have a balcony scene with Phyllis Calvert. When it came to the obvious line, 'Why do you love me?' I really couldn't say it because I felt such a fool. In any case, I wouldn't ever have qualified for that role.

Dubal: I saw a photograph from the test, and I thought you looked wonderful in your costume.

Menuhin: Well, certainly my children laughed heartily when they saw those photographs.

Dubal: I'm glad you had the chance to *almost* become Paganini in the film. But you certainly have played Paganini's music, and your performance of the D major Concerto has become justly famous.

Menuhin: That concerto is like Italian opera, and I have always loved Italian opera and Italian operatic style. I adore the freedom of the prima donna. I enjoy now accompanying prima donnas. It reminds me of when I first learned to drive in California as a boy of twelve and had my licence at twelve. I loved driving on the windiest and most impossible roads. I find the same pleasure today in accompanying a slightly erratic soprano. The two, driving the car along an unpredictable road and accompanying a soprano, it's something of the same kind of delight.

Dubal: After Rossini accompanied George II, the King said, 'Rossini, you are extraordinary. Nobody has ever been able to accompany me before.' Rossini replied, 'But sire, I would accompany you anywhere, even to hell.'

Menuhin: How sweet!

Dubal: It seems commonplace that writers still call Paganini the greatest violinist in history. Do you agree with that, and how do you judge something like that?

Menuhin: Well, I do agree with that, really, because he exercised a fascination which no other violinist before or since has equalled. Not only was he an extraordinary character and a unique phenomenon, he had a flair for what the public would be excited by. He knew how to present himself. But he was more than that. He was a genuine man of a certain, a great, integrity musically. His compositions, his Caprices, are admirable; they're beautiful pieces.

I think he has been underrated as a composer. Today we tend to say it's trivial music, but there is more to him that, and what he has contributed to the violin is remarkable. Of course, we must never forget that he came after a long line of predecessors who were very great violinists. When you begin with Vivaldi and you go on to Locatelli, Tartini, and any number of them, it wasn't as though he came out of the blue any more than Stradivarius came out of the blue. He and Guarnerius and Stradivarius, the violin makers, flourished all together because the violin at that time reached its apogee – it was the most important instrument in the world. It was louder than the harpsichord. Today the piano has become the loudest instrument, except for the trumpet, and the violin was the Italian effort to emulate the human voice, the singing instrument.

Dubal: Do you consider Paganini a tragic figure?

Menuhin: Yes, I do. My wife has collected the most wonderful portraits and billboards of Paganini programmes in England, and I've quite a collection of manuscripts as well, and he comes out a very tragic figure indeed. One of the portraits that I have of him is of his last years, when he looks so sad, so haggard, and so . . . a man who has really suffered a great deal. And I don't think anyone can play the violin that beautifully unless they have a soul that has gone through some torture. I'm sure that he had this incredibly intense, tortuous, dedicated and wild life. Well, not that wild, but he did have innumerable adventures. He was also very devoted to his son. He was a man who tried to lead a married life and didn't succeed, but he was an extraordinary figure in a day when people were extremely religious and superstitious. He evoked powers which were ascribed to the mythological, to the unseen, to forces which escape our control, to the devil, and so on. I see him as a tragic figure with, on the other hand, a remarkable grasp of financial matters. He was a frustrated modern concert virtuoso, touring virtuoso.

Dubal: Maybe the first great publicist as well.

Menuhin: Yes, he soon caught on. He was Italian, after all, and with that Mediterranean combination of heart and mind, of passion and wit and quickness of mind. He had a spontaneity which overcame everything. He must have been one of the most captivating people, and perhaps in some ways elusive.

Dubal: Your answer actually evokes for me Delacroix's great painting of him in 1831 when Paganini hit Paris with such impact.

Menuhin: Yes, yes. I have a wonderful English painting of him done a year or two before he died, and it is absolutely so tragic I can hardly describe it.

Dubal: Where do you place Paganini in the history of the instrument?

Menuhin: At the very highest point.

Dubal: Could a modern violinist today really be a violinist without studying any Paganini?

Menuhin: Well, of course he could, but I think every violinist should. Enesco introduced me to Paganini, and he made me play his music at a time when the D major Concerto was only played in the first movement, and then only in an arrangement by Wilhelmj. Enesco said I should play the whole thing. Of course, it was a colossal thing. I played a lot of Paganini, and I am grateful to Enesco for that introduction.

Dubal: Do you really believe at that time in big cities like Vienna, Genoa, or London that the 'in league with the devil' syndrome that Paganini was supposed to have was taken seriously? Did superstitions still run that high, that concert-goers could believe such a thing?

Menuhin: I think they probably did. They did believe in the devil, you know, and his powers. And of course, you know,

he wasn't accorded a Christian burial. And even today we are
not above superstition. Look at astrology. It's now the most
popular sport.

Dubal: Writers talk of the Romantic period and the phrase
'virtuosos as hero'. What does such a phrase mean to you?

Menuhin: Well, I think that was the time of the individual
who – whether it was Napoleon or whether it was Paganini or
people who by virtue of their sheer determination, ambition
and gifts – made a mark on the world. It was the beginning of
the capitalist era too. It was the beginning of the mass public.
It was the beginning of the time when publics were no longer
only the elite. And Italy was the cradle, after all, of the kind
of mass public for music.

Dubal: What are your opinions on the virtuosi after Paganini,
such as Vieuxtemps, Wieniawski, and did you have any
contact with the Joachim tradition?

Menuhin: Yes, I think that nineteenth-century violinists
after Paganini were romantic, passionate people. They were
composers as well. They hadn't yet become specialists. They
were as great violinists as any we have seen since. It was still a
time where creation and interpretation were not separated.
As for the Joachim tradition, perhaps Adolph Busch was
of the line. When I was a boy, Louis Persinger gave me the
Joachim concerto to study – a very long work. Is it at all
played now?

Dubal: Yes, the Hungarian Concerto. There are two recordings of the work now, one by Aaron Rosand. It's an effective
piece. He himself played it as early as Weimar with Liszt
conducting. Joachim was for three seasons Liszt's concert
master in Weimar.

Menuhin: I didn't know that. How fascinating.

Dubal: Who were the violinists you loved when growing up?

Menuhin: I was nurtured on Heifetz, Elman, Toscha Seidel and Zimbalist – all Auer pupils. When I was a boy in San Francisco, those were the ones, and those were the recordings I heard, particularly Heifetz's. I listened to him extremely carefully.

Dubal: Well, they scared every violinist. The very ideal of technical perfection which was attained by him was frightening.

Menuhin: Yes, I know. But I was determined to play the *Moto Perpetuo* and the *Dance of the Goblins* like Heifetz did, and with some time and trouble I managed the feat. Not knowing how, but I managed.

Dubal: Do you think Heifetz knew what he was doing to play on such a level?

Menuhin: Yes, I think he did. I think his great teacher, Leopold Auer, gave him a wonderful schooling. And it never let him down. What I admired was the sheer perfection of his control and the ability to turn out identical performances. I am not built that way; for me, each performance is an event which I want to live and experience as something special and unique. I can't be other than I am. But I do respect the sheer craftsmanship that predetermines everything to the last little iota.

Dubal: Somehow in his apparent heartlessness, there lurked a deep passion.

Menuhin: Oh yes. There was more than he allowed to reach the surface. I think he took great pride in control, and he was also a man who liked to control *everything*. He wasn't an easy man to deal with. He died, I'm afraid, with very few friends because he didn't have the flexibility, and it's a great pity because he's a great artist and I respected him.

Dubal: Let's talk for a moment about a violinist more elusive than Heifetz and whose playing you loved very much – Fritz Kreisler.

Menuhin: Oh yes, I could try as a youngster to emulate Heifetz in Paganini's *Moto Perpetuo*. But for me, something much more difficult to emulate was what Kreisler could achieve so effortlessly. Kreisler was the gentlest violinist I knew. As a person, he was as sweet as his playing. People loved him and melted when he played his own music. I realized when I heard Kreisler as a child in San Francisco, his music speaks of travel. His music speaks of other countries, other civilizations that I knew nothing about. I realized that someone with only a child's experience could not play like that. It spoke of manners, tenderness and other elements which I didn't know. Kreisler represented something you can't imitate; something that must come from life experience. What he had has to be lived. As a boy, I was a long way from Vienna, and a long way from that kind of sophisticated life. And it took me a long time until I could play Kreisler the way I needed to.

Dubal: Someone said such an elegance could bring a tear to the eye instantly and you would never know when.

Menuhin: Oh yes. And in 1936, in Paris, the time had finally come. I was twenty-one and there was no excuse not to be able to play *Schön Rosmarin* or the *Caprice Viennois*. I just *had* to do that or I would really be the most backward of children or young men. So I recorded them and the *Rosmarin* really stands up very well today.

Dubal: Probably the violinist with the tone that most melted the general public was Elman.

Menuhin: Oh yes, absolutely! I heard him very often. Everyone loved his tone, his sound. It was a sound that was irresistible, and so human. He loved to move on stage. As a boy I was so impressed because once he simply turned completely around while playing. He made a complete turn.

Dubal: Really no inhibitions at all.

Menuhin: None, he was really free, and he played beautifully. He was carried away completely. People would make fun of his slides, of his old-fashioned style. But he was inimitable.

Dubal: Did you ever play for Elman?

Menuhin: Actually, yes. As a boy, I was dragged down occasionally to play for eminent musicians. My father and Persinger and I came to Elman's very uninteresting hotel room overlooking Post Street in San Francisco. Persinger opened the conversation by speaking of Casals and calling him a great musician. Elman said, 'Oh yes, *but* he is only a cellist.' Then I played for Elman, the great man, and I can't really remember what the comment was, but the important thing was I was 'produced' for him.

Dubal: Let's speak of some performers that you have known or played with. Horowitz died in late 1989, at eighty-six. He was certainly the world's most celebrated pianist. Did you know him?

Menuhin: Oh yes, I even knew Volodya and Wanda when they were courting. I was nineteen when I first met him in Italy. I remember we took them out on a picnic, Wanda, Piatigorsky, my parents and sisters, and some others. But he really didn't want to come. He wanted to work. We used to go down often to see them in the evening. He practised all day – always. I remember one evening, he had practised the *Revolutionary Etude* of Chopin all day, and he wanted to show it off. He was sure of himself. He wanted to try it out. I never heard anything like it. It was really quite amazing. Here was a man who was concentrated on his keyboard as any human being had ever been. Horowitz had a genius of his own, in the mastery, in the touch, in the expression. He was driven, a driven man, by this instrument. He was possessed by it. This kind of possession is something we need in the world. We need people like that. The Russian artists, dancers and violinists also are possessed. This is a wonderful thing. Because there are certain things that happen in art only when you can give all and everything you have, including your life. Horowitz had this.

Dubal: In later life he didn't practise as much. But always more than he told people. But in his youth he served the piano's daemon well and there never was a harder worker, and he knew how to work wonderfully.

Menuhin: Yes, he was touched and tied to the piano, his life was geared to it. He was keyed to the keys of the piano.

Dubal: What about your sister Hephzibah, a true spiritual sister to you?

Menuhin: In every way we grew up together. She was my best listener. It was on her that I exercised my first rabbinical teaching, moralistic comments, and all the rest – musical too. She was the most wonderful listener, and she was such a dear person, and of course an extraordinary pianist. She had a particular gift for undramatizing. She didn't like any of the ordinary normal trappings of showing off. She was the most unegotistical in terms of producing herself – whether in dress or anything else. Diana would get her clothes. She had no desire to adorn. She was beautiful, and she was radiant, but she always underplayed herself. The French loved her playing. Everything was there, but there was a kind of sobriety in her playing. She hated exaggeration. She didn't even play wrong notes. Hephzibah had absolutely unbelievable command of the piano; she was a little like Glenn Gould, in the fact that she spent so little time on it, and learned a piece in no time. She played brilliantly, musically, but soberly. There was never a touch of exaggeration. It was all there, but it had to be discovered by a sophisticated public, that realized that kind of playing. I, of course, tried to bring her out emotionally to exhibit a little more. My other sister, Yaltah, was more poetic, more emotional.

Dubal: Was your frequent collaboration with Hephzibah satisfying?

Menuhin: Always satisfying, always, deeply so. Because we were like *one*. It was impossible for us not to feel like one.

Dubal: As a boy you were growing up while Paderewski was still playing the piano – a pianist who had been the President of Poland after the First War. Do you have any recollections of Paderewski? He now seems so distant from us.

Menuhin: By the way, his famous Minuet for piano was the first composition I ever played in public. My mother accompanied me. It was in San Francisco, at a YMCA. I met him once when I was a little boy, after a concert he gave in Los Angeles. I went back stage. He was a grand, grand man. He was one of the few moments when music and politics joined – as they can, especially in Central Europe. Music was so much part of that world.

Dubal: He indeed personified the artist as romantic hero.

Menuhin: He had style. He could play mazurkas and polonaises with incomparable style.

Dubal: Which brings to mind Paderewski's compatriot Arthur Rubinstein.

Menuhin: Ah, Rubinstein had style and panache. And enjoyed life. And made life very pleasant for those around him in conversation. He was very generous to my son Jeremy. He came to a concert in Paris, thought highly of him. He twice invited him for a whole day to his Paris house. Rubinstein had this old-world charm which is fast disappearing today. He was at ease, he commanded his world. He loved the good life, but in a balanced way. He pursued his pleasures, but gave a great deal to people, in person, and of course on stage, in one of the great careers in history. In his way, he behaved as an aristocrat. In the grand manner, with the due amount of selfishness which goes with it, and spoiled too. But he never abused it. He kept himself fit and elegant and sociable to a very late age.

Dubal: Besides your work with Hephzibah, have you had good experience with accompanists?

Menuhin: That is a world of its own. I've had very excellent companions throughout my career. My teacher Persinger played the piano well, and Enesco, by the way, was a tremendous pianist, as well as a great among violinists. Incidentally, Kreisler and Heifetz played the piano quite well. And in the world of the cello Slava [Rostropovich] is an amazing pianist. But yes, in my life I think Marcel Gazelle and Adolph Baller were superb, and also in my younger years there was Artur Balsam, a very wonderful musician. More recently, I played with Paul Coker, a charming companion. Occasionally I play with my son Jeremy, we have a huge bond between us. Life on the road is challenging, demanding and tiring, so you had better be in sympathy with who travels with you. After all, you eat, work and practise together.

Dubal: Did you ever play with Artur Schnabel – the king of Beethoven players?

Menuhin: Yes, I did – at Hampshire House. We played Beethoven sonatas together. He knew Diana better than me. He was rather a bore because he was so serious. He used to speak of active fatalism –

Dubal: What is that?

Menuhin: I don't know, I think something like you accept your fate or destiny but you do something about it. He was called the chairman of the Beethoven Trust. He was, of course, a marvellous musician.

Dubal: What were your impressions of Toscanini?

Menuhin: He was a real inspiration to me. Here in New York, I attended every concert I could attend of his. And thus I heard all the Beethoven symphonies, Brahms and so much else. That was a great education for me. I admired him enormously, and came to know him extremely well because we travelled twice by ship from Naples to New York and he came to my cabin each day and I played for him. My father once on deck had a talk with Toscanini, who told him that he closely arranged his time in the United States around the income tax laws. This seemed to impress my father, because he probably thought that a muscian didn't have any business sense. But in any case, he was a great musician, and love, passion and service to music was absolutely unyielding. He couldn't tolerate anything that wasn't his way musically. He was very demanding, and rightfully so. And even his famous tantrums were acceptable because they were in the service of music. They weren't personal. He was simply aghast if there had been something that didn't live up to his standards.

Dubal: Let's speak about Furtwängler the conductor. You must be sick of the political aspects of his career.

Menuhin: Of course I'm sick of all that. Furtwängler was a unique conductor. He didn't like beating, or bar lines – only wanted the music. Once when rehearsing the Beethoven Concerto, he loved the slow movement. He said, 'Remember the *same* tempo tonight.' Of course, that's a ridiculous thing to say, because some remembered the same tempo, and others played it with his tempo at the moment so the first bars were totally off. But he was a man who had to live his music;

he wasn't the cold, dispassionate analyser. Of course, he *knew* his music. He was a composer – an excellent composer too. You know I recently conducted in Vienna Furtwängler's Fourth Symphony, a very complex work. He was a musician in the grand old style – a master musician.

Dubal: What were your experiences with Klemperer?

Menuhin: The last time was when we recorded the Beethoven together. A marvellous musician, but I always felt he was a rough-cut diamond, as they say. He was rather vulgar and crude. Hindemith was giving a lecture, and at the end of the lecture said, 'Are there any questions?' And Klemperer, who was sitting in the front row, said rather loudly, 'Where is the toilet?' The stories about him are legion.

Dubal: I was reading something by Nadia Boulanger, a woman you revered, and she said:

> It seems to me that attention is the state of mind which allows us to perceive what has to be. It is a form of the vision experienced by the great mystics, on days when they were granted a profound concentration. Saint Teresa of Avila often comes to my mind. Great saint that she was, great spirit that she was, she still had what she called 'days of dry prayer', when she prayed and prayed – she never ceased to pray – but there was nothing! And then a day would come when she would hear. In art we call this inspiration. It is the moment when a man succeeds in grasping his thought, his real thought, right at the core; the moment when we touch the truth, when communion is established.

How do you achieve that focus, that attention and that communion which I think is the hallmark of your art?

Menuhin: Music makes that possible because you are in fact communing with the mind of the composer. I love to study the score and follow the mind of the composer. One is not only communing with the mind of the composer but with whatever the composer's inspiration was as well. Music itself facilitates such communion, and that's why there is always all over the world, in any religion and for any occasion, there is always music. Because it does weld the people into one feeling. Nadia Boulanger was a wonderful teacher, an extraordinary woman and she always stressed this matter of attention. She believed that you can reach that state of inspiration only if you attended to every little step on the way.

There are moments when everything is right and everything falls into place; but it doesn't fall into place unless one really prepared oneself for it.

Dubal: When did you meet Nadia Boulanger – perhaps the most celebrated composition teacher of the century, and a monumental musician?

Menuhin: I lost my heart to her immediately, as everyone did – as did my son Jeremy, who studied with her. She was wonderful to him. Anyway I was all of eleven when I met her, while I was studying in Paris. I remember the next year at a very grand party sitting next to her and discussing the C major Fugue of Bach for solo violin. Boulanger had a presence that had the firmness and granite security of the Rock of Gibraltar with the loving solicitude of a mother. Of course, this *grande dame* was a demanding person. She had a dedication to music that was indefatigable. She was highly rigorous, in music, and in the principles of her religion, she was a devout Roman Catholic. She was a fascinating example of the most acute French intellectual clarity with a wonderful Russian abandon and deep generosity – that part is so very un-French in its boundless exuberance.

Dubal: Just think of her influence on American composers. Copland, Thomson, Harris, Carter and dozens of others flocked to her. They adored her, and her influence on each was invincible.

Menuhin: And Nadia's contribution to my music school will not be forgotten. How I remember her uncompromising demands on the young students' concentration and self-discipline, and at the same time the inspiration she radiated. I personally made music with her over many seasons, and had her at my Festival in Bath, as well as in Gstaad. We played chamber music, she played piano, she conducted, she even brought her choir.

Boulanger, like Casals, believed in paying attention to up beats more than the down beats. The down beat, which is on the beat, makes its point more automatically, but up beats were an indication of will and decision.

Dubal: Did you know Casals well?

Menuhin: Very well. A most inspiring musician. Every note had to have a meaning. A man for great detail. I always likened him to a jeweller with a magnifying glass looking into a watch. He was also a man of conviction and passion, but he wasn't perhaps as big a man as he should have been.

I went to see him just after the war when he was living in the second floor of a house in Prades. He was very happy to see me. He played for me some parts of his Oratorio on an upright piano, and tears were coming down his cheeks.

He railed against Cortot, who collaborated with the Vichy government. But he spoke highly of Furtwängler. That was just after I had played with Furtwängler after the war, and I said, 'Why not do the Brahms double concerto?' 'I'd love that,' he said, 'because he's a clean man' – which he was. So anyway, year after year passed and I kept reminding him of his intention and promise. It would have meant a lot to Furtwängler, quite a gesture of reconciliation. And he finally wrote me a letter which was marvellously pure and naïve. He said, 'You see, I'll tell you why I cannot. I'm considered the leader of the anti-fascists, and in New York I have that reputation. And they wouldn't understand if I did a recording with Furtwängler.' Now that was a confession of a man who wasn't ready to live up to his conviction and believed that it was more important to keep his image untainted than to do what his heart dictated. And I was amazed at the honesty because a clever man wouldn't have made himself open. It was absolutely honest and naïve. He was admitting to a human frailty. And to that extent I don't hold it against him. The honesty touched me.

Dubal: Cortot, Thibaud and Casals formed a trio in 1905, and many people can never understand how or why Cortot became the Culture Minister under the Vichy government. Did you ever hear of any reprehensible act by Cortot?

Menuhin: I don't think he could have done anything really reprehensible. But what was reprehensible from the point of view of those who have survived the war under different conditions was of course that he took the job at all. That was held against him, and up to a point with justification. Viewed from the outside, it's easy to judge. Viewed from the outside, to take a job from the Vichy government is what one should not have done. But I'm always hesitant to go the whole way, because I know that so often the people who judge might not do differently themselves in similar circumstances.

Dubal: You cared deeply for Glenn Gould.

Menuhin: Oh yes, indeed. He was a man who lived very much within himself, having a phenomenal memory and a phenomenal command of the piano, and decided all audiences are superfluous to his art and he didn't want to travel anywhere. Glenn was a very North American character in the sense that he liked driving his car, that he loved the latest electronic gadgets and he followed the stock market every morning. He devoted every instant of life to creative thought, to music, to whatever he was doing. And whatever that would be, he would never be diverted in any way. He felt ill at ease with most people; he was very fond of Diana and of me, and we always saw a great deal of him in Toronto, but he always had an aversion to being touched physically or his privacy being invaded. I remember when we worked for a film, and I visited him at his apartment – it was a shambles. And I said, 'But you need a lady here. You really do.' Indignantly he said, 'Well, there is a lady who comes once a week.' I said, 'That's clearly not good enough, because it is a disgrace.'

Dubal: This is what women are for.

Menuhin: Not quite, but Glenn said, 'But if I ever found someone like Diana.'

Dubal: I want to quote you from your piece on Gould in a book about Gould called *Variations*. You wrote:

No supreme pianist has ever given his art and mind so overwhelmingly while showing himself so sparingly. This great phenomenon that was Glenn, a jewel produced by geological eons, presented a great rift in the continuity of the expected and the ordinary. Yet the similes are purely figurative, for he was an ephemeral presence and only the recorded echoes of his thoughts and passions remain forever to enlighten and inspire us. The key to successfully probing this phenomenon is Gould's essential creative nature.

Glenn Gould the creator, almost unwillingly trapped to a keyboard, was reduced to a recreative role normally filled by performing intermediaries attempting to entertain, astonish or bewitch an audience. So great were his dominating creative powers that they determined the structures and patterns of his life – one of the principal effects of which was his very private use of his time, of hours, seasons, and years. . . .

So great was the compulsion of his creative universe that he himself (the Glenn that one might but did not touch) was a very touching, tender and extremely sensitive, almost heart-rending, offering – a sacrifice on the altar of his own genius – for his fulfillment reposed entirely in the written and the tape records of thoughts and feelings in music and in words. . . .

Menuhin: Yes, he is an unforgettable figure.

Dubal: You performed with Gould several times in the recording studio. His view of recordings as a medium of art was the most extreme in the history of the invention; Busoni called it a devilish invention, but of course it has brought millions closer to music, and the improvements keep coming. Gould saw the recording process as the highest form of music making.

Menuhin: You know I once talked to Gould about the difficult question of reality versus verisimilitude. This talk was published.

Dubal: Some of it I'd like to reproduce here, because you both have valuable thoughts, which differ. You know Gould could spend a year on splicing, as he did on his second *Goldberg Variations* – which I call the *Gouldberg Variations*. How do you make recordings?

Menuhin: For example, while recording Beethoven's Sonatas nos 7 and 10 with my sister Hephzibah I completed an entire work, playing it three times without a break in the morning, like a concert performance, and doing the same in the afternoon. When we were done we simply told the producer to pick the best one. Recordings made in this way seem to me to have something immediate and compelling in them, which is lacking in recordings pieced together. Audio tape is a wonderful safety net, but acrobats are not re-engaged for the following season if all they do is fall and climb back up. Of course an obvious mistake should be corrected, for it can be tolerated in the concert hall as a passing disturbance, but if it were perpetuated in a disc it would no longer appear accidental.

Dubal: Yes, I agree. Let me continue with you and Glenn Gould discussing aspects of recording. You and Gould are listening to the playback of a Bach gigue, recorded 'close up'.

Gould: Now, Yehudi, you've got to admit that you would not be likely to encounter a sound like that in the concert hall.

Menuhin: I would still recognize your playing. Whatever you've added electronically does not add to the clarity and perfection, or the relationship of the voices, which is your inherent way of playing.

Gould: The point is that, if I were to play that piece in a concert hall, as I have done many times – in fact, it used to be one of my party pieces – I would not be free to select the perspective we just heard; it represents a tight, chemical, X-ray-like view of that work, precise and at the same time intimate, which enables me to dissect it in a special way. On the platform, I would be forced to accept a compromised perspective – one which would be more or less equally acceptable to the listener down at the tip of the stage and to the standee up beyond the far balcony. I don't need to tell you that, ultimately, one ends up with a perspective which is appropriate, if at all, only for the listener in Row L of the orchestra.

Menuhin: I simply play and the hall does the rest. But doesn't all this technology presuppose that the ideal listening point at home is one spot somewhere in the middle of the room? As soon as you have three people listening, two of them will be in the wrong place.

Gould: It is an absurd concoction when you think about it, because it means implicitly that in Germany the father will have the optimum seat, in America it will be the mother, in France the mistress.

Menuhin: I agree there is music today which demands the metamorphosis you can achieve on these amazing consoles if it is to survive. But the music that concerns me, the single-voiced violin, even though I sometimes play two strings or even three, is not materially affected by the choices available on that console.

Gould: I suspect that what inhibits you from making full use of the technology is the fact that it compels the performer to relinquish some control in favour of the listener – a state of affairs, by the way, which I happen to find both encouraging and charming, not to mention aesthetically appropriate and morally right.

Menuhin: You must admit the pianist starts out with an instrument which is remote from him to a degree. The sound is made through mechanical connections, therefore the electronic side is yet another mechanical manipulation, which is acceptable considering the vast spectrum the pianist controls. But the violinist's approach is intimate, personal, and this machinery appears almost as an intrusion. I believe both attitudes are valid. Splicing the tape, for instance, is what you feel enables *you* to achieve perfection.

Gould: I believe this whole question of splicing is a red herring; I think it's become all mixed up – and improperly so – with the idea of 'honesty' and 'integrity'. Naturally, it's antithetical to the concert process, where you go from first note to last, but that antiquated approach has nothing whatever to do with the major precepts of technology. It matters not to me whether I am 'successful' in creating a performance through one take, or whether I do it with 262 tape splices. The issue is simply not important.

Menuhin: You are building a structure corresponding to your vision, and anything that helps is legitimate. But take the Beatles, who started out playing in public spontaneously; by the time they became accustomed to crutches which enabled them to record tracks separately and put them all together, to add notes and take them away, they could no longer play in public, because the public expected something else, having become accustomed to this form of recorded creation.

Gould: In a sense, that is also what happened to me. I found I was competing with my own recordings, which nobody can do really. My recordings represent my best thoughts.

Menuhin: I refuse to believe that. I've heard you play, and I know that if you wanted to you could carry off a performance in the concert hall which would be as staggering as anything you do in the recording studio.

Gould: But doesn't it come down to this: If an actor wants to deliver a proper 'To be or not to be', he may do it in the context of the play *Hamlet*, or he may do a travelling routine in which he reads excerpts, as Sir John Gielgud used to do. In any case, he doesn't have to run through the first two acts in his head in order to find the appropriate tone for that soliloquy.

Menuhin: The point is that he must know the work as a whole inside of him, to know what it feels like even if he never performs it. There is a point beyond that, and that is that I often find greater satisfaction in reading a score rather than hearing a performance. You first have to hear it in your mind before you can play it.

Gould: But how do you explain the strange notion that the musician who sometimes happens to be a recording artist should be subject to different laws from the stage actor who may on occasion appear in films? It is quite legitimate for the film actor to have a series of emotive moments that appear to be in real time. The interior may be shot on a Hollywood lot, if such things still exist, and the exterior in Tierra del Fuego, yet the relationship between the shots is precisely what you do in making a record that satisfies your best thoughts on a work. They think it's fakery, cheating.

Menuhin: I think it is a confusion of two different worlds. The one is accustomed to living a thing through, which is the final result the public wants and considers real. Those who use techniques to enhance the dramatic effect would look upon the concert performance as old-fashioned, not taking advantage of the available means, and perhaps shoddy because people are satisfied with something less than perfect. Let us say a film about a mountain climber can be done in sections, a mock-up mountain can be used. The actor can take it easy, and probably won't want to go up anyway. But there is another risk – the danger to the climber who actually goes up the mountain and cannot do it in bits and pieces. He's got to do the whole thing as a consecutive effort.

Gould: Yes, but it seems to me that what technology is all about is the elimination of risk and danger. I suspect that this is where we really part company, because I don't think one should deliberately cultivate situations that have built-in elements of risk and danger, not if they can be removed by superior technology. That is the problem of the concert hall, where things can fall apart, the horn can crack, and so forth.

Menuhin: Has technology really reduced risk and danger, apart from music? Isn't there a risk of losing the sense of life, the sense of risk itself?

Gould: Obviously, technology has its own dangers, but I think the purpose of technology is to give the *appearance* of life.

Menuhin: Are you satisfied with the *appearance* of life?

Gould: Well, a recorded performance is not exactly real life.

Menuhin: So we have to live on two levels. When we satisfy a natural urge we can't do it in bits and pieces. It has its own built-in tuning. You can only stretch it to a point.

Gould: I can't agree. If your ideal 'To be or not to be' is something you carry around in your head, you might well repeat it to yourself one line at a time. Why then should you not assemble it as a composite, taking advantage of the benevolence that technology permits, the blanket of charity that it throws over everything you do?

Menuhin: I doubt this blanket of charity would evoke from the piano such playing as yours from anyone but you, with all the help it can give.

Gould: Compliments aside, why do you resist the idea that it is possible to cut in on a particular note and say, 'That is the mood, the tenor, the emotion behind that note'? It really needs only the context which one carries about in one's head.

Menuhin: On the other hand, once you've made the recording, are you sure you are not ignoring your listener to an extent? Are you sure he is listening to it with the same devotion and concentration as he would in the concert hall? He might be interrupted by frying bacon. In the concert hall there is something compelling; besides, certain types of music are communal experiences, for instance the *St Matthew Passion*. The whole congregation was meant to feel and react as one.

Gould: But it seems to me there is no greater community of spirit than between the artist and the listener at home, communing with the music. I would even go so far as to say that the most important thing technology does is to free the listener to participate in ways that were formerly governed by the performer. It opens up options he didn't have before.

Menuhin: That still doesn't invalidate the concert hall, the experience of which is essential, and remains the standard against which everything else is judged.

Gould: Nonsense. It was the standard until something else came along to replace it, which is exactly what the recording did; and the recording, surely, is now the standard by which the concert must be judged.

Menuhin: If no one is ever going to climb a mountain again, and we have to be satisfied with films about it, where are we?

Gould: We are without people who can climb mountains.

That, I think, is a profoundly good thing. It will save any number of deaths per year.

Menuhin: No, you mustn't say that. You'll make up with ignoble deaths on the road.

Gould: If I had the technology to prevent them, I'd do that too. I'm sure it will come.

Dubal: Gould truly did desire the listener to be more than a consumer, to become a participant. He wanted what Copland called 'the gifted listener'. I once wrote that Gould would have loved to present his public with Glenn Gould kits of all his different takes in the recording studio, and let the listener put together their own Glenn Gould performances.

Menuhin: Well, that's a fascinating concept. Glenn really believed in his way. He retired at thirty-two years old, and I doubt anything could have brought him back to the stage. But there is no denying the quality and quantity of his recorded output. There is no body of work quite like his.

PART TWO

On Music and Life

Dubal: You wrote your autobiography, *Unfinished Journey*, in 1975. What are a few of the significant happenings since that time? You are now seventy-five.

Menuhin: Fortunately, it's still an unfinished journey. I've added to my grandchildren – Jeremy had a second child recently. The days are always full. Certainly my return to Russia after being more or less banned for seventeen years, returning under the regime of Gorbachev – I can't begin to tell you what an emotional experience that was. The emotion of the audiences, my colleagues, and to hear that marvellous language, and feeling the ferment – to see those new tender shoots blossoming – I truly hope they are not to be trampled upon brutally underfoot. It's very promising.

Dubal: Of course, I'm a little bit sceptical about all this new *freedom*. It has always seemed to me that the human family has done its best to escape from freedom.

Menuhin: Yes. That has been its course. But there seems to be some room for faith now.

Dubal: Verdi said, 'To have faith is good, to not rely on faith is better.' Do you think that Gorbachev, one man, can liquidate an empire in a week and give millions of people so-called freedom?

Menuhin: But it's come not as the work of one man. It's been because of those brutal and terrible years. It's been building up through the poets and writers – especially in Moscow. This could not come as a result of one man. Therefore, it has come at a ripe time. The people have been waiting for it. It's been boiling up, and I'm sure it has been planned for a long time.

Dubal: The world sees you as having lived a charmed life, but how do you see yourself?

Menuhin: I agree with the world opinion as far as the charmed, lucky and fortunate life I've had. In fact, my life today is an effort to express the luck I've had. First of all, parents who *really* cared about their children. They instilled in us a faith in life. We had good habits, regular work and plenty of fun. My sisters were marvellous companions. The timing in my life was very fortunate. Growing up in San Francisco was wonderful because it had an *endearing simplicity*. A child could grow with less tension. Of course, I saw San Francisco from my ideal child's eyes. There were many injustices, such as with the Chinese, who were not allowed to bring the women along, would often work for years to accumulate a little savings and would have it stolen off them as they left the country. But as a child I was oblivious, and to me it was a paradise.

My parents had a house, a garden. The mortgage was $50.00 a month. I'd sleep on the porch. My parents then rented some rooms to help with the payments. We had a little car – my grandmother helped us with $500 to buy it, which only cost $800 then. We lived most comfortably on $300 a month. The rest went towards my violin. Then I was fortunate in travelling to France by the age of eleven – getting to know that language and to be with, as a child, Adolph Busch, Enesco and so many others. These were inspiring speakers, teachers as well as great musicians. Even when I was five and six, I was blessed with a teacher of the quality of Louis Persinger, who not only taught me but played the piano in my early recitals. He was a student of Ysaÿe, possibly the greatest violinist of his age. Persinger brought to one a great tradition. At four years old, I knew from his sweet sound that he would be my teacher.

Dubal: It seems that all of your salient traits were visible from childhood – all was instilled early. The tremendous worker, the fine use you make of different environments, even the great physical as well as mental discipline was established by your parents and teachers. Life seemed to come to you. When you eyed a Stradivarius when you were a boy, it came to you as a gift.

Menuhin: Yes, imagine. In 1929 when thirteen, after a long tour from coast to coast, I played the Tchaikovsky at Carnegie Hall. I had dreamed of playing on a Stradivari called the 'Prince Khevenhuller' which I had seen a year before – of course, there was no chance of us affording such a treasure. After my concert – that might have been January 1929 – I was made a present of this violin by Henry Goldman, a patron of the arts. I was overjoyed. I took this instrument on my second European tour and used it for my Berlin debut.

Dubal: Such a thing can hardly happen today. The patron seldom gives to individuals anymore.

Menuhin: Exactly right. Now institutions receive the gift because of tax deductions.

Dubal: Hans Christian Andersen, talking about an 1842 concert that Liszt gave in 'mercantile' Hamburg, wrote that Liszt, the performer, saw people in their Sunday spiritual dress, even in the wedding garment of inspiration. How do you feel about the public from the musician's vantage point?

Menuhin: I think the performing musician is a very fortunate person. People are there to listen – listening, however, has taken a back seat in our civilization to seeing. It's now almost totally a visual civilization. We judge things by their aspect and not by what are the vibrations inside them. Seeing has a certain objective, but it is also a distancing from the human material, the object from life. With the audience, if they are able to follow the music, the inner vibration as it is happening, to feel the music as it is happening, one is then really seeing the audience in the best possible light. That is of course if they are approving. I also, through my observation, feel that women listen better than men.

Dubal: Your celebrity was so world-wide. Were you ever spoiled or felt superior?

Menuhin: Absolutely never. I owe that to my parents and to music. One cannot be spoiled except by the most trivial and superficial aspects of life. After all, I wasn't playing the violin to make a fortune or anything else. I played the violin because I wanted to play the violin. I studied with people who had very high ideals, so the plaudits of the public or critics could not replace the fact that I was playing for the music. I was and remain a pygmy, as it were, if I compare myself with Enesco, or with some of the great conductors I have known. And besides, the interpreting musician is always subservient to the composer. So there was never a moment I felt superior. I know I'm not. I remember I was a rather cheeky little boy. One day in San Francisco, one of the great elder powerful ladies that ran San Francisco came up to me and said, 'You are just like Paganini!' whereupon I said, 'Well, have you heard Paganini?' I wasn't susceptible to flattery then, and I'm not today.

Dubal: It seemed that any time you really needed something formative to happen, it did.

Menuhin: My only merit is that I have not tried to command time. The best things happened by chance, not as a result of direct effort, but as third and fourth repercussions of taking advantage of an opportunity, through curiosity, love and desire to understand. It's not by going directly after the thing. That doesn't lead very far. The shortest way, I have always found, is the longest way in time. And the longest way is by far the most interesting, rewarding and shortest. It's the way there, it's what you learn on the way. And if as a young man you are given all the wealth in the world and the fame, and didn't know anything about it, it would be suicidal, it would be a mortal blow.

Dubal: Aldous Huxley once wrote, 'The marvellous thing about music is that it does so easily and rapidly what can be done rather laboriously in words or cannot be done at all.'

Menuhin: Quite right!

Dubal: Walter Pater said music is the art that all other arts aspire to. Mendelssohn said music is too precise for words. I suppose he had this in mind when he wrote his 'songs without words'.

Menuhin: Yes, of course you can't give orders in music. You can't say, 'Sit on the chair.' Nor can you give statistics. But you can communicate what only poetry can communicate, that is the real direct contact between the emotional, the spiritual moods. You just can't do that through words. Words are too devious; words leave too many opportunities for misinterpretation; and even if you are exact, often words kill the spirit. And of course there is more to words than words.

Dubal: Yes, and often the word is not the thing described. There can be a great distance between the mere word and the complexity of the object – a chair can possess many attributes other than the word.

Menuhin: Yes, indeed. Even how a word is said. I think if you can invest words with what music *has*, so that the words themselves only become a transmission, a vessel of something more than the exact words. Each of us says something or writes something which contains an element which is totally unintelligible to someone else. I wrote something – and soon find out that someone interpreted it as quite different from what I meant.

Dubal: I suppose the chief word here is 'interpretation', which Henry Miller called the most important word in the language. Even in long relationships, people often find out how frequently they misunderstand each other. Relationship is moulded by words.

Menuhin: Oh yes, that's right. We are misled by all these so-called exact sciences and by things that are tangible, by such things as dictionaries, which give meanings. And yet words are almost meaningless when they are meant to convey love or trust. Legal documents cannot convey these things. Words are constantly being formulated by lawyers which are unintelligible to anybody. They imagine that they have secured reliability, and all they have done is convey a contract which possesses no relationship – and we imagine by using words that we can convey feelings.

Dubal: Even in music set to poetry, music almost always dominates terribly the text. Many poets hate their work set to music.

Menuhin: Yes, that's right. Almost always. You know, I always like to think when speaking with someone that I have to feel and think the right attitude. Then the words have a chance of saying something.

Dubal: That is a magnificent concept!

Menuhin: We may have a common language whatever the language may be. But it's still a long way from the common language on which we base those words. And that can be either personal, communal or regional.

Dubal: And of course literature, as soon as it's translated, is in big trouble. One translation from one era can portray an entirely different concept or even fashion. I was looking at various translations of Goethe's *Faust* and they were disheartening to read. Sometimes a phrase was laughable and silly, and another translator would see the same passage as lofty and noble. Can you imagine Beethoven using the language of words rather than music?

Menuhin: No, not possible. Beethoven actually had trouble in communicating in words. The late quartets are beyond our comprehension of words.

Dubal: Yes, the mathematician J. W. N. Sullivan called those quartets 'States of consciousness'. He felt that even Shakespeare never wrote his C sharp minor Quartet.

Menuhin: Yes, this work shows us what areas of communication Beethoven at the end was pursuing.

Dubal: Berlioz, who heard the first Paris performance of the Quartet in C sharp minor with only a few people attending, wrote to Liszt, I believe, asking him if this Beethoven was of the same species as the rest of us.

Menuhin: How very interesting, and how perceptive Berlioz was. The notes in music are nothing, unless the musician really knows what the notes mean. I was just conducting the Beethoven Fifth. So many conductors make it over-pompous. The usual way is a sort of 'Destiny Rings'.

Dubal: It's much more than military music or 'Fate Knocks at the Door' – there is great anxiety in that work.

Menuhin: Yes, so if such a work is filled with anxiety, that must be conveyed to the orchestra people in ways beyond the words. And the interpreter has to go so deeply. It's like finding and following clues, and gradually finding the answers. Little clues which are not in the score except to the extent that you must use your analytic powers based on the notation. The moving from one mood to another, and this moving must be in a fraction of a second, and yet the whole thing must be in one flow. As if you are always speaking. It's a time art. And of course, the joy is in the improvised and the unpredictable. Without these, we would have no interest at all – in life or music. Therefore, while playing a work for the first or three hundredth time, the fascinating element is the extent to which it lives, therefore the unpredictable – and yet it must be predictable. It's extraordinary that as soon as the focus is upon the instant, the living instant, the audience feels it and knows it. There is a vast difference between that and simply a mechanical performance of the notes. I long ago realized that what I was looking for was the distortion. Like the improvisers of jazz. They work against the rhythm band; the rhythm band goes day and night whatever happens, so that the improvising part is free to improvise. The rhythm goes on, no one loses their count. When I look at a score, I'm more interested in the distortions. The not measurable. But the distortions should be clearly thought out in advance – which notes should be longer, shorter, louder, softer, which is the high point – then it should all be rubbed out. And what's left gives a plastic contour and depth. This is what is fascinating in fashioning phrases.

Dubal: Yes, without this fluidity, one realizes, with its division into whole and half-steps, how limiting Western music can be.

Menuhin: Yes, it is very limiting, until you realize that it is trying to say in its own language, rich or poor, things that are universal, with its own method of communication. I think once you get *that* into your head and realize that it's a living substance like a river flowing – and that it can be guided within limits, navigated, it is not flowing at a metronomic pace – then it suddenly comes to life.

Dubal: This is not in the notation, even with the best attempts of composers.

Menuhin: No, but it must be deduced from the notation, no matter how limited. But of course one can play the notes and it can mean nothing.

Dubal: What is a true teacher?

Menuhin: I think a true teacher is one who is ready to learn. It's not sufficient to do a thing – even passably – oneself. But to be able to live with the student. To understand their potential, to choose the key element which may turn the whole thing around for them, if they are ambivalent. To also be able to find their weak points, to find their strong points. It is a long, serious process for the teacher to uncover and unravel the student's potential. Let's remember that many students have been harmed irrevocably by their teachers.

Dubal: Many teachers are such only in name. The harm they do lives after them, and daily. Most students spend years trying to overcome their teachers who have egos, the equal of the most terrible prima donna's. I love this passage written by Madame de Staël in 1810. She says of the omniscient teacher: 'And where shall we find tutors willing to give twenty years to educating one child? That kind of care and attention would compel every man to devote his whole life to the education of another being, and only grandfathers would at last be freed to attend to their own careers.'

Menuhin: What a superb quote. It's such an exacting task to be a teacher. It requires a special attitude of humour, of lightness and seriousness, or sympathy. It isn't necessarily true that those who can play can teach, and it needn't be the other way around either. I started my own school to try to pass on some of the things I received from my great teachers, and also to say that I went to school, which I didn't.

Dubal: Perhaps that was one of the advantages in your life, not going to school. It can be an enormous waste of time as well as frustrating for a gifted child. Edvard Grieg was asked about his school years and his reply was simply, 'School brought the worst out in me.'

Menuhin: I know what you mean – and for me not going to school was in some ways an advantage, no doubt. It was compensated by all kinds of things, such as travel and meeting all kinds of interesting people. But the lack of schooling was not compensated for in the ways of practical human contact. I didn't develop that necessary and essential technique or gift of assessing people in the practical way – at least for some time in my life. Because I saw them as ideal people, nor did I ever expect anybody would be less than absolutely honest and true. So a little experience finally made me understand that people can unite in themselves various qualities, good and bad, in the most remarkable way. And there *are* evil people. There are such. They are conditioned to that. But on the whole, I feel it is important to trust people. I'd rather trust people generally than distrust them. For one thing, it's more pleasant – it's much easier. And the risk one runs is minimal. If you distrust people you run constantly a risk. Trusting people you only run the risk of once in a while being mistaken. Which isn't too bad. However, there are people whom I definitely by now know I can't trust – I do not see life as they do.

Dubal: Your own school has been very successful. This must please you enormously. Anton Rubinstein, who founded the St Petersburg Conservatory, said it was by his school that he wished to be remembered.

Menuhin: I well understand that. You know, I hated the word 'prodigy'. It made one feel abnormal. That's one of the reasons I wanted to start my school. I like to think of myself as normal. Perhaps I was wrong, perhaps I am a monster. All those musical children are normal children who should have a wholesome environment. I think children are vastly under-rated. I think children are capable of much more than we expect of them in their early years.

Dubal: How should the study of the violin proceed?

Menuhin: I believe that violin study should begin and concen-trate on the early Italian violin composers. Education today does not follow the chronological sufficiently. It now proceeds in an egocentric way. People today who study want to play whatever they love, right away, whatever it be – Tchaikovsky or Brahms. This is a kind of ready-made answer, which in education should be avoided with children. They should be presented with the same problem that people had when they looked on the flat earth. Why is it round, and how do you explain it? Let them find out the premise. The violinists would understand more about their instrument if they pro-ceeded with the early works. Pianists are more consequent with their progress.

Dubal: Yes, they get their Bach early. Von Bülow called Bach's *Well-Tempered Clavier* the pianist's Old Testament. And before that, they study the Two-and Three-Part Inventions.

Menuhin: Yes, indeed, and pianists even get their Bartók early in the marvellous *Mikrocosmos*, whereas the violinists immediately want to play whatever it is they fancy. Not only should violinists begin with the early Italians, and even vocal study, they should be very early introduced to jazz, impro-visation and dance.

Dubal: Improvisation has died out. Young people are terrified of it. As for becoming free, nothing is better than dance. I had a dancer come to my Piano Literature classes at

Juilliard where he improvised a dance for twenty minutes to the Liszt A major Concerto, then I had the whole class dance and make up their own steps. The confusion was terrific, but their inhibitions started to vanish.

Menuhin: How absolutely wonderful! I think that's terribly important. We have separated dance from music. We get only rhythm, a blank, noisy hardness with no music in it. We live in a day when so many elements are divorced from each other, and they needn't be divorced if they meet on a high level.

Dubal: I am amazed at this sterile specialization which is so ruinous, and uninspiring. Occasionally I will take my Piano Literature classes to the Guggenheim or to the Metropolitan Museum. I tell them that they can learn a great deal about colour in music from the great painters. I tell them that Schoenberg painted and drew and so did Busoni, Gershwin, Granados, MacDowell, and so many others. That simply practising like robots won't make them artists, and yet most of them prefer to not go, but to stay in the school and practise. Guilt is so entrenched in so many instrumentalists that they feel miserable away from their instruments.

Menuhin: Yes, I can't tell you how much I understand.

Dubal: What about the idea of having to publicly report a concert?

Menuhin: Well, they say it's good for general standards, but isn't it also a threat to spontaneity in performance? To feel your performance has to be written about is not always comforting.

Dubal: Why should performers have to feed critics? Perhaps some of the salary of the newspaper critic should be given back to the performer instead of paying the tax to the government – the performer's retribution.

Menuhin: I like the idea – I have always felt a certain ambivalence about the subject of criticism. After all, concerts have gone on during long newspaper strikes and nothing seems to be lost. Folk music and tribal dancing has gone on for ever without any reviews in the morning newspaper. And then critics are so often pedantic. They like to report an out-of-tune note or notes missed, or memory slips, to show us they know the score better than the average concertgoer – but seldom give such details in their full context, making them irrelevant.

Dubal: How do you view the critic's role? Have they done you more good than harm?

Menuhin: Oh, I think critics definitely have a place. The best of them are extremely well informed, write well and put their finger directly on the spot. And the public needs and deserves some sort of guidance in matters, and a report. Where the critic is unable to judge is when it comes to reasons *for*. Because they are not always capable of going into the psychology, the emotional condition, the approach of the individual. They can judge results, up to a point, but they cannot judge causes. When they try to give a cause, they are generally totally wrong, and that's in the nature of things.

As far as causing me harm or good, I think I must say that generally they have only been beneficial; not only because I probably got infinitely more good notices than bad ones, but also because I think that those that are critical might very well have a point. I am my own, naturally, most critical critic. I know very well, and so do most musicians, especially in these days of recordings and so on, we are accustomed to hearing ourselves. Just as women looking in the mirror are well aware of all their blemishes, so is a musician hearing his recording well aware of all his weaknesses. I think that the critic, if he is honest, if he isn't seeking to show off himself or to demolish, I think where the critic can be of crucial importance may be in judging a debut recital. Even then, I mean there may be other chances, but that's where it counts for most; where the public doesn't yet know the artist, and where the critic may have the opportunity of either enhancing a career, pushing it on, giving confidence, or perhaps rightly saying the artist isn't ready yet.

Dubal: Confidence is wonderful, and of course encouragement is the best thing any teacher can ever give to a student.

Menuhin: Yes. On the other hand, you cannot encourage someone who is on the wrong track.

Dubal: That happens with much teaching.

Menuhin: Yes. I know that I am generally not inclined to be ruthless or hard, but when I feel that I am put in a position where no one else is going to say the truth, then I've got to say that. I mean, many times young people come and play, and I am all for their pursuing music, but not necessarily as a profession. I think it's much more important really to love music and then do something else, and keep on playing and using it as an amateur would use it. That is by far the nicest use of music anyway.

Dubal: Arthur Loesser in his book titled *Men, Women and Pianos* wrote:

> At the height of the reign of technology, only those things that machines can make the fastest and in the greatest quantities can command the fullest respect. Good machines must give way to better, those that make things for a million are thrust aside for those that can produce for a hundred million, while the supplying of mere thousands becomes an act of charity or of eccentric devotion. The logic of the machine, then, colors all sense of values and all ethics of human relations. People acquire not what they might want for themselves, but what machines can most conveniently and profitably

make in the largest amounts. A man no longer apes his betters; rather he strives to be one of a great majority, one of those for whom the machines can do their best. At the climax of the worship of technology, its priests say 'mass' – using a word that pretends we are not men, but crumbs in a pile of the inanimate stuff that machines live on.

Menuhin: That's very interesting. Loesser is perfectly right. Because the mass propaganda, the mass opinions, which are generally based on ignorance and prejudice and superstition – these are still very much the order of the day. There is very little information – real knowledge, for instance – in many of the disputes that are taking place today over theoretical issues and practical ones that lead to laws being made. It's generally the majority. Whereas truth is neither obligatorily of the majority nor of the minority. Truth may happen to be a majority opinion, it may happen to be a minority. It may happen to be only one person alone; after all, Galileo didn't command a majority opinion, and yet apparently he was right. But I'm sure Darwin didn't command the majority opinion. And by the same token, I think that we have to find the happy medium between majority and minority opinions and truth, which may not be of the one nor of the other.

Dubal: Yes, truth is elusive. William James said, 'The greatest enemy of one of our truths may be the rest of our truths.'

Menuhin: How extraordinary that statement is. Truth is something outside of us of which there can be many varieties, and of which there may be a central core that is generally true; and we make each our own truths which can be dangerous, because there is this genetic quality in us, which demands individuality and would like to make each of us unique, while in a mass civilization, like today, it produces freaks like Hitler – freaks who achieve uniqueness by an uncontrolled ambition for power and are very clever in some particular way to get it.

They don't have to know a great deal, they don't have to be philosophers, but they have to have an instinctive feeling for what the frustrations of the nation are. As soon as they can cater to those, as soon as they can point to the devil and promise anything, they can command.

Dubal: I'm going to read a passage from Alan Watts, his autobiography. Alan Watts was a philosopher who wrote books on Zen and so forth. He said:

> The trouble with industrially civilized people is that they have no gift for spontaneous music. Our music is so counted out, scaled, metered and trickily calculated, that no one but an expert may have the nerve to indulge in it lest he be accused of making a nasty noise. But we would understand the sense of life if we could sing more and say less.

Menuhin: Quite right. One of my ambitions is to see every school day begin with singing and dancing, just as the Kodály method has been introduced into Hungary, to the great benefit of the scholastic levels of the students. They breathe better; they have a better sense of community; they are more relaxed; their circulation works better and they are more alert. I think that would be an excellent thing. But he is right, Watts, about the effect of industrial society. It's a society where everything has to be planned in advance; where the most rigorous timing is now part of our lives; where every second is calculated. And therefore, we are in fact trying to compensate, looking for spontaneity. We resort to all kinds of ways and means, and I think that we feel very intensely this lack of spontaneity, which has again to be cultivated, because the human being cannot afford to be just spontaneous. The only way he can be just spontaneous is to be violent. That is, of course, the quickest answer; that's the immediate answer. Frustration and suffocation and rigorous discipline, as methodical army drill, may very well lead to violence, but on the other hand we need discipline. What better form of discipline than music, to both create the *self*-discipline which is necessary, and the spontaneity? We are having this great trouble with freedom altogether. We can't get to terms with freedom. Either we abuse it, or we deny it. But we cannot find the real balance, because in *ourselves* we have lost the ability to blend spontaneity with discipline.

Dubal: How are we, as a human family, going to get this back? Because without this co-ordination of values, we're in trouble, we're out of touch.

Menuhin: Yes. I think we can get it back through an understanding and a sympathy with the human being if we have above the discipline the desire to be of use and to help and to respect the past and to prepare for the future. The trouble is so often that discipline is merely used for immediate results, immediate gains, at the expense of the future, at the expense of the past and at the expense of others. As soon as we can get this element into our calculations, that we are really here to be of use to our fellow men, I think that the element of spontaneity will come through the gate of compassion and sympathy. And then of course vibrations are what connect us to each other. We are all part of what vibrates throughout the universe. We are part of everything. We couldn't survive unless we had in fact something of every element in the world. It's only by suppressing ourselves, by destroying part of ourselves, that we feel we can survive in a world that doesn't understand anything but either the drive to power or the commercial drive. In other words, either it's propaganda or it's advertising, and the two are not remote from each other.

Dubal: And we feel manipulated by both and often broken from propaganda and commercialism.

Menuhin: Many years ago, when playing in Detroit, I was staying with a very fine gentleman who was the public relations man for American Motors. During a break, I had stopped practising, I looked around his library. It was his study. I took out a few books and manuals, on public relations and advertising. I realized what I hadn't realized until then – that the size, the technique, the art, whatever you want to call it, the psychology of advertising and of propaganda was exactly the same. And the total contempt for the public, and the way to manipulate its thoughts and its desires – the technique was exactly the same. And that America having been far more advanced in advertising, and as a result of the study of psychiatry and psychology and all the rest, understanding how people are primed by their innermost ambitions; to be free, to be happy, to enjoy companionship, to enjoy love, to enjoy power and all the rest – that these techniques may have very well served Russian propaganda, because they learned a great deal from America. I wouldn't be surprised at all that they took some lessons in American advertising.

Dubal: I would like to talk a bit about science. Let me read a tract by the English writer Thomas Peacock, who was born around 1780 just as the Industrial Revolution was exploding. This was written in 1825.

> Science is one thing and wisdom another. Science is an edged tool with which men play like children and cut their own fingers. If you look at the results which science has brought in its train, you will find them to consist almost wholly in elements of mischief. See how much belongs to the word 'explosion' alone, of which the ancients knew nothing. Explosions of powder mills and powder magazines; of coal gas in mines and in houses; of high pressure engines in ships and boats and factories. See the complications in refinements of modes of destruction, in revolvers and rifles and shells and rockets and cannon. See collisions and wrecks and every

mode of disaster by land and by sea, resulting chiefly from the insanity for speed, in those who, for the most part, have nothing to do at the end of the race which they run as if they were so many Mercurys speeding with messages from Jupiter.

Menuhin: This is very good!

Dubal: Yes. I'll continue.

Look at the scientific drainage which turns refuse into poison. Look at the subsoil of London; wherever it is turned up to the air, converted by gas leakage into one mass of petulant blackness in which no vegetation can flourish, and above which, with the rapid growth of the ever-growing nuisance, no living thing will breathe with impunity. Look at our scientific machinery which has destroyed domestic manufacture, which has substituted rottenness for strength in the thing made, and physical degradation and crowded towns for healthy and comfortable country life in the makers. The day would fail if I should attempt to enumerate the evils which science has inflicted on mankind. I almost think it is the ultimate destiny of science to exterminate the human race.

Menuhin: That's *absolutely* wonderful, and how prophetic. And there we've been doing it for 170 years since then, going on full tilt. Of course, many people have learned that we have damaged, incalculably, the world. Whether we can retrieve any part, I don't know.

Dubal: How do you feel about the United States now that you are *Sir* Yehudi Menuhin?

Menuhin: There is such a store of vitality yet in this country. More than anywhere. You come to this country with renewed hope. And despite the efforts perhaps to control, America is still largely a wild and uncontrollable country, and that is its saving grace.

Dubal: But that uncontrollable part scares me.

Menuhin: Yes, but it's its saving grace. People who refuse to be controlled are capable of great things. And people who have such vitality are capable of change. The capacity of accepting the better, the element of wildness . . . I mean, even if the worst came to the worst, the rest of the world would be obliged to preserve the United States as the wild zone for humanity – the sort of place where people can still be what they are. Not quite what they are in the jungle, but at least each person here can make his own life. He can also break it, and the penalty is very high. But he has still the capacity to break the mould and to respect the past for what it is. This country needs inspiration and guidance and high ideals. For other countries, that wouldn't necessarily suffice. But this is still a country which, with all its practices, is still at heart innocent.

Dubal: Yes, it is. That is amazing. How has it retained it? Is it the constant influx? Is it the amount of ideas here? Is it the one language from coast to coast, three million square miles?

Menuhin: I think it hasn't had time to absorb so much and to crystallize such a variety of population. It has allowed its people to develop instinctively. Some of them may be rough, questionable characters – I don't know. But they are still human beings who are all, for the most part, redeemable.

Dubal: What are a few thoughts on the British and India? Elgar's music for me is the height of Edwardian luxury. In the slow movements of his symphonies, I must say I smell imperialism – Kipling, India and all that.

Menuhin: Yes. Well, it was in the air. But I don't think there have ever been any more innocent imperialists, and any that did it more for the sheer exuberance of it. Really, there was very little sense of national ambition, pride, control. Look, they ruled India with comparatively few people, leaving the Indians to their own devices, except that every maharajah had a British adviser, and he had to do what the British adviser suggested. But the system, the structure, was left intact. Meanwhile, they got roads and parliaments, hospitals and trains.

Dubal: And Steinway's pianos were carried in on elephants. But I think your fondness for the English is getting in the way of history. How can there be innocent imperialists? The world is still paying for England's former glory.

Menuhin: I know that they had their horrible excesses; they did horrible things. But if you compare it to other empires, it was by no means so virulent.

Dubal: Yes, it's hardly Cortez mounting Montezuma.

Menuhin: Exactly, not that at all. The Spanish went at it for sheer greed. The British, when you know the British, you know that they travelled to India to see the world, and India fell into their laps with a trading company. It was trade. It was trade, and it was adventure. Because they lived on an island, surrounded by water, and they had to see where the water went to and they went as far as the water took them. It took them to strange lands which they wrote about, they painted.

Dubal: Perhaps because they are physically large, they needed to get off their little island.

Menuhin: Not only that, but they loved to travel. They didn't have cameras. Many British drew, and drew beautifully. They were cultivated people who went with their pencils and drawing boards and crayons, who brought books along and who read. Not many of them, it must be said, in all honesty, appreciated the Indian culture. But there were a few who did. There were a few who did translations from the Sanskrit. But the middle class, who then came to fill the ranks of bureaucracy and the trading, they put on airs; they had to feel superior. It's always those who are newly arrived who have to feel superior. But those who are superior, by either social position or breeding or heredity, don't have to exercise it.

Dubal: It seems that good conversation is today at a minimum.

Menuhin: Generally speaking, you are correct. But of course, it depends with whom one talks. If the subject is interesting and the person is authoritative on it, then, of course, it may not even be conversation in a strict sense. It may be an exposition. And then there are other conversations that are delightful in the give and take, such as with diplomats and statesmen who are dealing in affairs that are not strictly verifiable in the scientific sense, but are totally verifiable in the human experience. Then it leaves way for a playful, as it were, shedding of light on different aspects of a problem, according to each person's private experience of that problem, whether it's poverty or peace or war or social conditions. Then there are conversations that tend to take place with me that are often of the uninteresting type, when people say, 'I heard you when you were five years old,' or something like that, which is very sweet sometimes, and which doesn't lead to a conversation unless I deliberately prolong it and ask certain things or ask what that person was doing at that time or were they already interested in music? The conversations that I like most would be conversations that bring me – selfishly, that is – information that I didn't have before.

Dubal: Are you upset if a conversation is non-productive or banal?

Menuhin: Most conversations are, of course, of no value. Occasionally, a person speaking is so enchanting that you

98

don't mind if they discuss trivialities. Because even trivialities and gossip, if it's not malicious, can be quite amusing and entertaining.

Dubal: Of the great musicians you have known, who was sparest with words?

Menuhin: Bartók, I believe, who was an extraordinary man who never said a word that wasn't essential. And of course, that led, especially in our babbling society where everyone talks a great deal, and usually loudly, to a sort of stalemate, because Bartók, in the rare times he was invited out, would often contribute nothing to the conversation at all. And for Americans, that's very disconcerting.

Dubal: Yes, Americans often feel uncomfortable if there is any silence between people. Listen to American radio, where there is never a second of rest. What about England in this respect?

Menuhin: I think it is still perfectly possible in England to sit in a railway carriage with five other people and not talk. You aren't expected to talk. Or you can sit in the car with someone driving you, and he won't break the silence, whereas in America one has the feeling that you must establish a communion, you must establish some contact, even with a stranger. You might say something about the weather, but you might also say where you've come from in the United States.

Dubal: And soon comes that most odious of invasions which begins, 'And what do you do?'

Menuhin: That comes quickly, although I am always embarrassed about that. Because I wonder what business is it of mine, and why should he do anything? Why shouldn't he just be enjoying life, and contributing in his own way by not doing, by going and visiting people he likes, or doing some work without pay, or being an amateur at something, or why should he justify his existence? Why must people justify their existence by saying, 'I work'? I think we must change that, especially in light of the millions of unemployed.

Dubal: And many people are embarrassed to answer that question; there's so much expectation in this culture of status related to what you do. Perhaps this filling a vacuum between people is due to the vast number of telephone calls that goes on constantly, and the moment someone says 'Hello,' one must *go.* The words have to flow. But getting back to your statement about justifying one's existence, do you think there is a particular group of people who seem to need to always justify their very being? Do you feel you have to justify yourself? Responsibility seems terribly important to you.

Menuhin: People should not have to justify their existences. The Jew has a certain feeling that he has to justify his existence. He carries in him a kind of burden. He has to prove before God, or the rest of the world, that he has a reason for living. There are millions of people – bless them – who don't carry that burden around, raise good children, and live good lives. Some of the young musicians today are some of the nicest people in the world. They are so different from the old form of ambitious musician – you know the type – make a career at all costs.

Dubal: How can we utilize the constantly growing army of the unemployed? People need to work, to be useful; without that, they die.

Menuhin: The unemployed don't have much money, but they have leisure, and many have skill. And when you look at the cities about you, when you look at the people, everything is in need of care: painting, roofs, repair, children looked after, taught languages, music lessons, dentistry. There is no end of work. Now, my scheme is very simple. You would have people who would inscribe themselves voluntarily, saying they would be ready to give so many hours a month in their profession. Whether they are retired, whether they are eighty years old or twenty years old – whatever they may be – whether they play the violin or repair shoes or make shoes – whatever it may be. And that list is in central clearing houses – all you need is a voluntary secretary and lists – that each region or each block or each group of ten city blocks would have. And other people would put themselves down for – one hour would be equal to one hour. That is, there would be no money involved, and no one saying, 'Oh, I'm a French teacher and worth twice as much as a garage mechanic.' No, one hour of service per one hour. And that would be outside the moneyed economy. Certain materials would have to be provided, no doubt. The manufacturers might give a certain percentage of their products to this out of the goodness of their heart. It would not interfere with the regular economy, because these would be jobs that no one could afford to attend to otherwise, and the people would remain unemployed.

Unemployed people today, at least for the most part – I know that there are people who starve, even in this country (no one who starves in England) – nonetheless, the motivation is much stronger in this country. But, those people have leisure. Leisure to do what? To be of use to your fellow men and to study. It wouldn't matter if they went fishing; it wouldn't matter if they had wherewith to fish; it wouldn't matter if they studied Greek, or if they taught painting. As I say, any, any job. But the face of the country would be lifted as far as the appearance of the people, their houses, their clothes. Everything could be done with millions of unemployed who would not starve themselves, and who would be of use to their fellow men. This seems to me such an obvious thing, and there is already a beginning of that. There is a lot of that going on, but it isn't yet on the huge scale it should be. Unions would be silly to oppose it, because they wouldn't stand to gain. As I say, it's like my LMN, you know, Live Music Now, which I started in London. Now it works in France, Spain, Belgium and Holland. It is bringing together 90 per cent of the population that never goes to concerts, and cannot anyway – the concert halls couldn't accommodate them even if they tried to – or cannot go because they are too poor, too distant or too infirm, or whatever the reason. Ninety per cent of the musicans, who are excellent musicians, coming out of conservatories, who find it difficult to make a start in a career. They play in prisons, hospitals, factories and department stores, clubs, at weddings, at funerals, and so on and so forth. They earn a little money; they get to know the population; they live privately. Private people learn to know what a musician's requirements are – it has innumerable valuable side fruits. But this would be an extended form of LMN which would apply to every profession. Projects like this would heal the community and bring people into closer contact, and bring about this compassion and this health that I am speaking of.

Dubal: Do you think that in evolution, when the human brain suddenly expanded and enlarged, that there was just no time to smooth out the biological animal being in us, which became united with this new technological brain, and because of this, we have become a mentally ill species?

Menuhin: But yes, man is by definition mad. We *are* mad! And there can be a holy madness; it can be great madness – Schumann was mad and so was Baudelaire. And many other artists are mad as well. Yes, the human race is surely mad. The brain developed incredibly in man, largely because he suddenly discovered that there was *choice*. But we exercise choice already in the abstract – I mean, we think of things and exercise choice. We can construct in our minds whole cities and whole symphonies without ever setting them on paper. And every note represents a choice, dictated by the whole context. And as soon as you have a choice, your brain has to take into account alternatives. And I think the fact that we can conceive of many alternatives and then have to make a choice has increased our brain capacity by multiplication by, you know, $2 \times 2 \times 2 \times 2$ to the thousandth potential, which is a number which we can hardly conceive of.

Dubal: Have you noticed that we seldom memorize anything? For instance, the tradition of learning speeches of Shakespeare or poems from memory is almost over. This is almost eradicated in our educational system, at least in the United States.

Menuhin: I think that's terrible. Memory is one of our greatest gifts. It enables us to live, to survive, and without memory we'd be nowhere. And this is one of the essential faculties which should be cultivated at school. I think every day we should learn something from memory that we recite. That was the great advantage of the civilizations that had no writing. Everyone was educated, in the sense that they all knew their sagas or holy scripts or their great laws; and there are still traditions of that – such as people going around India reciting the great saints. They carry the whole *Bhagavad-Gita* in their heads. And they're considered as saints and given free food and shelter wherever they go, because they're bringing the people their great heritage by their memory.

There is a wonderful film, *Fahrenheit 491*, which depicts the totalitarian state in which all books were banned. They were all burned, and people went around memorizing the classics.

Dubal: George Steiner said that as long as we possess this oral tradition in our heads, we can never become 'zombies'.

You know, Hans von Bülow, a despotic and brilliant conductor of the second half of the nineteenth century, demanded his orchestra to stand up while playing and often had them memorize the score.

Menuhin: Really! But how interesting! You know, you're telling me something which I've often thought of. I think that's wonderful. With all these televised performances, the most disturbing feature is there is really nothing communicated to the viewing audience from musicians who look at their music stands and their sheets.

I remember seeing a television programme of Lenny conducting the 'Eroica' with the Vienna Philharmonic, and his expression was of Jesus on the cross. Bernstein was suffering in the Funeral March as if he were being crucified, and it was very touching. Perhaps some people might find it exaggerated, but it is certainly genuine. I adore him. But then, when the camera turned to the trumpets, all you could see on their faces was the expectation of *the next beer*. And it made such a silly, ridiculous juxtaposition, of the conductor really feeling the music and the others just playing the notes.

Dubal: I remember seeing that exact thing, and I saw Lenny in ecstasy and in despair, and I saw those orchestral faces looking more dead than alive.

Menuhin: So, it struck you the same way? Well, you'd find that in many orchestras. But I do think it would change matters if they were playing from memory.

Dubal: And, you know, it would bring something that is crucial to music again, and music-making – which is a rapt attention to the music, and they would look like they loved the music. Nothing is so rapturous as the look of a musician playing without a score – behold, inspiration!

Menuhin: Yes, yes, yes!

Dubal: May I now ask you something completely different? Are you a vegetarian?

Menuhin: I am very much a vegetarian. I don't eat red meat. I eat fish, I hardly eat other meat. My wife is more a vegetarian than I am. I feel that I don't need meat; it doesn't help me.

Dubal: Yes, and also most animals are, thank Goodness, vegetarians. There is no need for us to have meat. But we develop the taste.

Menuhin: Yes, but certainly we should eat much less meat than we do – much, much less. Not necessarily out of humanitarian grounds, but simply because it saves the soil. We can produce much more nourishment, the equivalent nourishment on less land than it takes to graze animals. Besides, the animals today are fed with such poisonous materials, antibiotics, and every other thing, not to speak of the battery poultry, which is a disgrace. We would have to change our diets. We have to change many things. And that is where the need to reconcile freedom and restraints is going to be a very crucial thing. There will be those who will preach their fanaticism at all costs, and there will be those who will preach and practise restraint at all costs. These are great issues which are going to become more and more crucial as the years wear on, as the months wear on. Because everyone must realize that we cannot continue at this rate, at this rapacious rate of using the resources of wood and forest. It is a disgrace. There again, what is more important – a few acres more trees, or an issue of some magazine? And that's where again our electronic gadgets and radio and television can perhaps bridge that gap of information to a certain extent. Awareness, and also the information that the newspaper brings, perhaps they might bring without the need of the newspaper itself. Maybe we can see printed-out articles we want to read in a way that won't destroy our eyesight – which television now has a tendency to have an adverse effect on. And maybe we can improve these things so that we won't have to level areas the size of small countries every day. I mean, the destruction is such today that we will not ourselves survive the destruction of our forests.

Dubal: Knowing what a fine awareness of nutrition you have, how do you avoid all the terrible food you are exposed to on tour?

Menuhin: For one thing I certainly wouldn't drink that soda you have been sipping. Just read the label – there must be forty different chemicals.

Dubal: Yes, I know – you always give me a certain look when you see me drink this junk. But lately I've changed my ways. This is a regression.

Menuhin: Well, I'm not about to tell you what to drink, but that stuff is poison. But on tour, I bring in as much as possible to maintain my self-sufficiency – for instance, bran, wheat germ, fruit, yogurt. I like bread made with wheat, rye and barley, breads with raisins and nuts and, yes, bean sprouts. I order in my hotel room a fish, fresh vegetables and always salads. The more I travel through America, the more I'm convinced that it is a suicidial society. Thousands of food products are truly hazardous to your health.

Dubal: What are the foods that you think of as valuable?

Menuhin: Well, I have a whole shopping list which I have printed in my little book, *The Compleat Violinist*, where I also have photos of the many exercises I do. The body of a violinist must be as in tune as the fiddle. Anyway, I'll give you a few items on my shopping list. The first being wheat germ, wheat bran, plain yogurt, honey, bone meal, fresh fruit, organically grown if possible, kelp, molasses, cider, vinegar, soya oil or thistle oil, which is the lightest oil. Ginseng, vitamin preparations, and so on. I am also extremely interested in Chinese medicines.

Dubal: It sounds very healthy indeed! Do you ever get colds?

Menuhin: Ah, if I ever sneeze, I take a German preparation called Medvitan, very useful against colds. It's taken by injection and painless, I give myself an injection of Medvitan.

Dubal: I've looked through your exercises, and many of them are also particularly good for violinists, such as strengthening exercises.

Menuhin: I'm a great believer in exercise, but those which are natural for the body, and of course breathing exercises are ideal for relaxation.

Dubal: You used to enjoy driving automobiles.

Menuhin: Growing up I adored driving in San Francisco, of course. The roads were not yet crowded. I still like driving in the country, and I used to love driving in Paris. Because Paris, you know, didn't adopt the red and green lights until after the war. There were hardly any red and green lights in Paris at all; it was a free-for-all. So you'd approach a crossing, a street corner, hooting your horn, and sort of sniffing out if someone was coming to meet you. It was really a game. The Arc de Triomphe, it still is to a certain extent. It's a game, finding your exit and your entry. But I loved driving in Paris at that time.

Dubal: Was life much simpler around 1925?

Menuhin: I can tell you that San Francisco used to be my dream city. The city water in New York was the most pure and crystalline, the most wonderful water imaginable. It came straight from the mountains. It was the best city water that any city could ever boast of. But San Francisco was a wonderful city – beautiful, clean, people very friendly, neighbourly, good community feeling, very clean – it really was a dream city. Now if the wind is blowing the wrong way from the Richfield oil refineries, the air is polluted. There's still enough wind coming for the most part from the west for the air to be rather better than most cities are. It still is wonderful, it still is a romantic city. But it has lost a great deal of that simplicity. The San Franciscans used to put a knapsack on their shoulders and go Saturdays and Sundays hiking. I don't suppose many people hike today. But the whole city, it seemed to me, was out hiking over the weekends. It was a very simple civilization. The automobile had just come in, there weren't so many automobiles, and there were still electric cars. Very elegant ladies in lace-draped electric cars – the windows were lace-draped – going up the very steep San Francisco hills, very slowly but relentlessly, as San Francisco women are. If only the gasoline engine had waited upon improvement in the electric propulsion, we'd have had a different civilization, in one way anyway.

Dubal: How do you feel about the draft and military service?

Menuhin: Well, I think the general draft can be a good thing. Conscription could be a good thing if it were a contribution to the enlightenment, to the sense of service, if for famine relief, which we spoke of, community service, learning trades, and so on, as they used to advertise the army service, and defending your country or your alliance or the world civilization against – for instance, when the Falklands issue came up, the whole of the world was behind England, the Security Council to a man. Obviously, England was in her right. I mean, it was an attempt by the Argentines to take over by force a bit of land that didn't belong to them, however near it was to the mainland. All right, there was the opportunity for Margaret Thatcher; there was the moment when she should have said: 'There is no international organization to prevent this kind of attack on defenceless people. Look at the Russians in Afghanistan. We will do the job, and I hereby place a quarter of the British navy and the army at the service of an international organization, where I would expect a quarter of the American, a quarter of the Japanese, a quarter of . . . to serve this purpose so that these are always standing by to prevent such aggression.' Well, that was her moment; that was a great moment missed.

Dubal: Do you think she ever thought of such an idea?

Menuhin: I don't know. I don't think she did.

Dubal: I think Santayana – someone – said that if we don't learn from the past, we will be condemned to repeat it.

Menuhin: Yes, we always repeat mistakes. People just don't seem to learn. They have more means, and they use those more means to repeat on a bigger scale the same mistakes they've always done. The bomb has certainly made us, and must make us, very quickly mature. Because, for the first time, we cannot allow a war to happen. We have not outgrown our thirst for victory. We still somehow prefer victory to peace. Because peace means work, peace means compromise, peace means understanding your neighbour, your opponent. Peace means helping your enemy. In peace, you must live with your neighbour or try your best to understand your enemy. But we'd rather really be victorious over our enemy. We'd rather squash him and not hear from him anymore. We want the hundred per cent victory. In the next war, there won't be any victory parade. But we can't be impatient with the past either, or else we would have to chuck everything out. The baby with the bath water, as they say. After all, we wouldn't be here but for the past, and we wouldn't have trees, flowers, grass and birds but for the past. We must keep the past in balance and understand it deeply.

Dubal: I once said to someone, 'Oh, what a shame that the library at Alexandria was burned.' And he said he didn't think so. He felt that almost all the books there must have been superstitious junk. He felt that those books were worthless dogma and that they were holding humanity back.

Menuhin: Oh, but what total nonsense! Those books contained the knowledge of thousands and thousands and thousands of years!

Dubal: So you think it was a horrible moment, that fire?

Menuhin: Oh, horrible. And as there were no copying machines, those manuscripts were unique. No, it wasn't junk, it wasn't junk. It was the whole knowledge of medicine, astronomy. No – it took seventeen hundred years to make up for that fire. We had to learn so much all over again.

Dubal: What are your feelings on the French Revolution, with all that equality and fraternity?

Menuhin: Yes, indeed. All right, the rights of man. The Greeks knew about the rights of man. What did the revolution bring to the French but disaster and more tyrants, and soon Napoleon, an extraordinary man in his way, but who became a tyrant and who brought to France more emperors.

Dubal: How come after the revolution everything deteriorated so quickly?

Menuhin: I think it liberated a huge popular expression which gave the mob its voice. It was then led by the herd keepers, by the false shepherds, and it released an energy which produced the leaders of this mob. That is the problem, because you have to have different leaders depending upon the quality of the mob. When they are slaves, it is a simple matter. But when you lead them with slogans, that is a slightly higher level where you have to justify and promise. The French Revolution was bathed in blood. I don't defend the stupidity of the monarchy, but they were simply not prepared for such a disaster. They went as far as they could go exploiting and didn't realize they were creating enormous pressure for a reaction which would culminate in the revolution.

The guillotine was a great invention. It was the first time that death was made so mechanical. And until then, it was a personal job. They had to use axes and nooses and it wasn't very efficient. The guillotine was a turning point in the history of organized murder. A true product of the Industrial Revolution, clean, efficient and almost painless. And very *modern*.

Dubal: What role should an artist play in society?

Menuhin: I don't like to define any role. There are artists completely immersed in their work – poets, musicians, painters. Why should one expect them necessarily to take any position? I don't believe in an imposition of one's particular life on anybody else. I think it's one of these ways of feeling superior – he should do that or he doesn't do that.

Dubal: What are good aspects of democracy for the artist?

Menuhin: The opportunity of not being tied to a particular form of ideology, being free to express every kind of good and evil, every kind of style he sees around, simply communicating with people and expressing his reaction.

Dubal: Is it possible that music as an art may be a fulfilled art now, and that music after 1915 has no relevance to the large public? Music's greatness was satisfied, it seemed, by 1910.

Menuhin: I don't believe that, because I continually see works of value.

Dubal: Works of value, yes – but what about great works, the works that have survival power?

Menuhin: It's difficult to tell now; it takes time to understand new works, especially today, where each composer is not a part of a school. Once you know the school, then, for example, if you know Mozart, you can understand Haydn. But if you know Bartók, you don't necessarily understand Stockhausen or Berio. But there are marvellous works written.

Dubal: Rilke said that there is an essential aloneness to works of art.

Menuhin: Yes, certainly the artist, when he is creating, he is totally alone. No one can create for him. It is the height of individual existence, of uniqueness – there's no question of that.

Dubal: Think of science. The creativity of the individual genius, like Newton or Einstein, is obsolete – to get to the moon needed teams of gifted scientists.

Menuhin: Exactly. That could have never been done by an individual. On the other hand, works of art can only be done by the individual.

Dubal: Perhaps there will never be in science another Einstein, because science has become so collaborative.

Menuhin: Yes. But it still doesn't exclude the one man who will suddenly see the light, and see the *obvious*, because it's the *obvious* that eludes.

Dubal: The obvious is usually oblivious.

Menuhin: Absolutely. That's well said.

Dubal: You've been fortunate to know so many people, including that legend of the painting world, that great scholar who taught us to truly see Florentine art, Bernard Berenson.

Menuhin: He was the uncrowned king of Florence, a little man in his late eighties to nineties when we knew him, and a real up to a point wise Jew, and not without a touch of vanity, very spruce . . .

Dubal: Some say an overwhelming vanity.

Menuhin: Well, you know, I understate. He was good

company, marvellous to talk to, he understood painting
better than he understood music, but he liked and appreciated very much when I played. When I thought it would be
nice to spend a little time in Florence, he gave us another
farmhouse on his property where we stayed for two years.

Dubal: Did you learn anything about painting from him?

Menuhin: No, not very much. He was very fond of my wife,
Diana. They had a correspondence every week or two over a
period of years. He was very active and walked as long as he
could, and attributed much of his lightness and flexibility to
the fact that he walked on mountain paths where you had to
dodge stones and roots and so on. He liked that very much.

Dubal: On April 12, 1929, you played your now celebrated
Berlin debut. Albert Einstein was in the audience and said
after you played, 'Now I know that there is a God in heaven.'
What is your conception of God?

Menuhin: Well, at my debut Einstein, I think he was rather
ecstatic. But he must have been the kind of man who knew
that there was some power, some order, something greater
than human. We call it God, but that's an anthropomorphic
conception. It needn't be anything two-legged with a beard.
I am sure it isn't. But it is some basic order which is not an
order as we see it. It is an order in time that evens things out.
Hot becomes cold, cold becomes hot, dense becomes sort of,
you know, vague, like the Milky Way, and other stars are
formed. The constant flux of cause and effect and of always
opposition, two sides. And we ourselves are two-sided, and
leaves are two-sided, and forms – musical forms – have
exposition and recapitulation. Those kinds of basic rules of
the universe. Einstein must have been aware of them, and
was in fact searching for some basic law that would include
gravity and electric magnetic attraction. He already was one
who saw that energy, which is the opposite of mass, could be

combined in an equation, which of course is the height of human philosopy and conception.

And today we must see that the destructive and the constructive have to be reconciled. We cannot say that we must forever banish the destructive, because we cannot. They are part and parcel of the same thing. In Indian mythology the same god is responsible for destruction and creation, which is quite an interesting concept. But we have tried in our Christian way. I say Christian because through two thousand years of Christianity we have tried, and succeeded to a certain extent, in separating good from evil, and I don't think it is basically possible. We have to see the two as part of one, and therefore seek to make the best, and turn evil to good; but not to say, 'He is evil and I am good.' Because that's not possible; we are all sharing the same evil and sharing the same humanity. Sugar is an example. We have separated the sweetness out of all products; whereas when we eat anything, we eat our sugar. But by making pure sugar, which doesn't belong to any substance any longer – whether it's made of beets or sugar cane – you can't trace from what it was made; it's just pure sugar, like a chemical. Because we wanted pure sweetness. And we can mislead every horse and dog with pure sugar. And the same with pleasure; we are looking for pure pleasure. Well, life isn't like that; it doesn't give us pure pleasure. But we are trying to lead lives exemplified by Hollywood's view of the high life, the good life where there is pure exaltation of leisure. Which in fact it isn't. Such a view is always full of disaster.

Dubal: It always will lead to pain very quickly.

Menuhin: Oh yes. But until our education comes to terms with evil and with pain and with death, and with the resurrection of the spirit, until we see life as a cycle, as a continuous cycle, we will remain rather childish and limited.

Dubal: Are these differences in personality traits of orchestras – say an English orchestra, a German or a Russian group?

Menuhin: Yes, there is a team spirit, the wonderful way in which the English orchestra differs, say, from the German. If there's a problem the German orchestra will await the conductor's guidance, and he will resolve the problem. On the other hand, any problem that can be solved by the section in an English orchestra itself will be solved with no burden on the conductor at all. They get together, their fingerings . . . Well, if I want a particular fingering, then I ask them to try it, and it may or may not be better than the ones they are using, but they will always sort out their own problems in each section. One has to also learn to treat them – well, I would anyway – with the respect that is their due, because they are such wonderful musicians. They have such a sense of style, whether you are doing Mozart or Bach or Stravinsky. Furtwängler used to prefer doing *Tristan* with the Philharmonia orchestra than with the Berlin Philharmonic. He adored England. And Toscanini preferred the BBC to any orchestra that he knew. The English musician is quite remarkable. He is very quick. He sight-reads remarkably.

And one has to also know how to handle them at rehearsal. I was rehearsing with Ivo Pogorelich and he was doing the Tchaikovsky Piano Concerto, which he has done since probably before he was born. His wife, Alicia Kezeradze, had come to see me the day before because he was detained by an air flight delay in Yugoslavia. So she came and went through the concerto, telling me exactly what he'd like. So I thought I was prepared. Then at the rehearsal, he did some different things. I said, 'You know, I only did this because it's your own wife who told me that's the way you did that.' But that's not the point of it. The point of my story is that we were rehearsing, and then at one time he said, 'Look, this passage is so passionate and so emotional and tragic. And the orchestra is playing it so coolly.' I said, 'Well, you don't quite understand. We're rehearsing it to determine how we are going to play it. However,' I said, 'just be patient.' I addressed the orchestra and said, 'Look, we have with us a wonderful pianist who was trained in the Russian tradition, and they, you know, go full out, twenty-four hours around the clock. Whether they are rehearsing or giving a concert, they always give all they have. It's not our way, because we like to reserve it for the concert. But let us play this passage as he would like to hear it now.' So we played it, with all the passion – no Russian orchestra could do better than that. And he was very happy. So I said, 'Now you know how it can be, and how it'll be this evening. Now, let's go on working.'

Dubal: But how did he get away with getting *his* performance? Most young pianists hardly get their way with a conductor.

Menuhin: Yes, hardly. But there was a good *entente*. He accepted too. And I naturally feel, having been the soloist all my life, that the conductor's job is to follow the soloist and to humour them.

Dubal: I have sometimes noticed that although Russian players are admirable in their technique and temperament, they have a rigidity about new ideas. For instance, I said to one young Russian pianist, 'Why don't you just feel free to improvise on the piano, make some sounds?' She said instantly, 'Oh no, the piano is a beautiful instrument. I don't want to make ugly sounds.'

Menuhin: Yes. Well, it depends on the training, you see. It has been so very thought-out, so methodical. The Russian method is very demanding.

Dubal: But this does breed a certain kind of rigidity.

Menuhin: Yes, it does. And then if you fail at a certain time, pfft! You go back to the beginning. It's really something which in the Western world we could hardly take. But those who survive are, of course, very remarkable. The rest go into orchestra and so on, which is again something which we could never accept. An orchestra musician is often a great musician. But in Russia, somehow the hero: soloist, the Tsar, the dictator. They've never known an enlightened civilization; they've never known a democratic civilization. How should they be other than they are? They've just continued the Tsars.

Dubal: Patience is perhaps more in the Indian character than a Western trait. Patience is, it seems to me, one of your virtues.

Menuhin: Yes, but it's not passive patience. My patience is really a kind of dogged patience. What it is is faith. I can be patient if I'm convinced that I am on the right track and something is happening all the time which is eventually going to yield the right fruit. Then I can be patient. I cannot be patient with things that require total resignation as the Indian can. Their patience is of a higher kind – perhaps it's passive. I can be patient if I know that the thing is cooking quietly, simmering on the stove, and will be ready in six hours, six years, or six decades, or perhaps for the next generation. But I want to believe that it's on the right track.

Dubal: Well, yours is a creative patience.

Menuhin: And then you must have faith too that it's going to be one day right.

Dubal: So your patience is part of a flame of discontent, really.

Menuhin: Well, it's a matter of faith. I can have the inner feeling, of hopeless or wrong. I feel, for instance, the few things I've proposed, I know they're right. I can't believe that they're wrong. And yet I know that they're not going to happen probably in my lifetime ever. So I cannot afford to, I cannot storm the powers that be – you have to accept that. That's something difficult if you know that people are suffering at the same time.

Dubal: Do you think of such things as reincarnation or an afterlife of a kind?

Menuhin: I do believe that there is continuity. I don't know of any way of defining it. I don't believe it's a primitive continuity that consists in having everything we would have liked to have had here, there, only better. That surely can't be the case. But I do believe there is a continuity in motion – we know that. And there must be a continuity in genes – we know that, too. And we know that we bequeath our children certain things. Whether there's a continuity actually in spirit I wouldn't know, but we have to live in that ignorance.

Dubal: And living in that ignorance has always been lonely for the human race.

Menuhin: Yes, they'd like to be assured. The human race wants always to know that the earth is absolutely flat and you can't fall off it. And it's not moving, God forbid, *it mustn't move.* And what has shaken the human race as much as anything is the knowledge that *everything* is moving. That we are moving, that nothing is permanent, that the humans one day will disappear, that the earth one day will vanish, and that the solar system will crumble. That is very difficult for the human being. What he's striving for all his life is to assure that his children will inherit what he has, that tomorrow is going to be planned and take place as it's planned. And therefore, he is singularly unprepared for the unexpected. You will find that people on the eve of a war will still be going about their little tasks; the Jews in Germany, who continued living under Hitler and couldn't believe what he had written in his book and what he had forecast, what was being done during that time, right in front of their eyes.

Dubal: And they call it a holocaust, and that word is totally wrong. A holocaust is something that moves very quickly. This was very slow, year by year for centuries and for the Nazis.

Menuhin: Yes, this was very, very deliberate, very planned. And that is what makes it so terrible, because we will accept killing in the heat of war. But the planned genocide is horrifying.

Dubal: The human animal begs for security. Fear is the major emotion.

Menuhin: Yes, we don't know from now to the next moment whether we will survive. But you have to live with some sort of inner calm and faith.

PART THREE

On the Human Condition

Dubal: The idea of countries is now a very, very primitive idea. Nationalism is a major scourge. These frontiers are so arbitrary – Bartók was born in Hungary, now he would be a Rumanian.

Menuhin: Yes, they're very primitive. I feel nationalism is at best a compromise. The boundaries . . . look at African boundaries drawn in Brussels – straight lines through a continent with no reference to geographical, tribal areas, no reference to anything human, no reference to ecology. And there they were, ruling the Congo and ruling other areas, which brought these areas, you might say, very far ahead, if you want progress in terms of technical advantages and knowledge and schools and hygiene and all of the rest. But at what cost? I feel that we have reached the point where with a computer we can afford to be infinitely more flexible.

I know that I am speaking of a time which is far removed from our own day, that I seem to be speaking of Utopian considerations. And yet I think in some ways that I am more realistic than others, if only for the reason that the realism that the others believe in is the violence that is destroying us. And therefore I believe that there are many superimposed communal areas that needn't conform one to the other. For instance, if you are speaking of meteorology, well then you don't speak of nations, do you? You speak of *global* weather conditions. It's not one nation that makes or breaks the weather.

All right, well, you need a global entity to represent meteorology. No single national element can do it; that must be a co-operative thing over the whole world. Then you speak of, let us say, Alpine flowers and Alpine growth.

Well, that is something that would encompass France, Italy,
Germany, Switzerland and Austria. All right, there should
be, just like we had when we built the dam in the South, a
commission that looks upon the whole situation concerning
the waters, from where those waters come, the Tennessee
Valley Authority. Well, there should be an Alpine Authority, with authority to look after Alpine flowers regardless
of what nation had it. The Rhine is another example where
nations should have no say. It doesn't correspond with national
responsibility. That belongs to Switzerland, Germany,
France, Holland, but it belongs also to the whole of Europe.
It drains Western Europe. Therefore, it again requires an
authority which has a different regional district and shape to
that of Alpine flowers. They may overlap. The same thing
applies to culture. The culture of borderlands belongs to
each of them, whether it's Hungary and Rumania, or whether
it's Germany and France with Alsace and Lorraine. These
require a different treatment.

Dubal: Are we perhaps in a transition era to a new awareness
where we shall save ourselves and this beautiful earth?

Menuhin: I think so. But unfortunately, we don't have as
much time as we need. That is the crucial point. I think we
have burnt so much of our time behind and ahead of us, that
it used to be that we could never do so much damage as might
destroy the whole earth. Now we can.

Dubal: Now we can. One more big war, and the great experi-
ment is over.

Menuhin: Yes, and when it comes to pollution, look what's
happening now. More and more quickly, more rapidly in
succession. The nuclear disasters – already there's a continuous nuclear pollution which results in leukaemia and
certain forms of cancer, which occur in areas of low pressure,
like St Louis, more than other parts of the country, because

that's where it gathers. And we are continually subject to this accumulation, this progressive accumulation of poisons, which are that much more active when they are working together – the food poisonings, the chemicals, the nuclear wastes, and so on and so forth. So that we are going to be faced more and more with situations which demand, catastrophes which demand immediate action for which we are unprepared. These will occur more and more in rapid succession. That's why the statistics that extrapolate a certain population by a certain date I think are wrong. Because it'll be some catastrophe, if not war, that's bound to attack us long before we reach those figures, I think. But it's something that requires urgent action, and yet all our sense of urgency is directed to issues which really are not relevant. We are fighting nineteenth-century and cavemen issues at a time when they are in fact no longer relevant, because other issues are much more important. But the important issues we are not attacking at all. We're still fighting in terms of who's going to win the next war, as if anyone is going to win the next war. We're still thinking in terms of who is going to get a piece of land or to protect a boundary or a frontier when it's no longer relevant.

Dubal: No longer relevant; only our survival now is important. When will we grow up?

Menuhin: Exactly. And people are fighting, as they've always fought, simply out of bad habit.

Dubal: There must be a world-wide death wish. A worldwide indifference to life. Even smoking is a death wish; the package says *you die*, but smoking is on the increase. We are overpopulated, but babies are being born by the thousands every minute. The 'right to LIFE' groups are part of the death wish – quantity, not quality of life.

Menuhin: Yes, there is a death wish – and I know what you

are saying. We must decide to do something about it. That's why, when I'm asked whether I'm pessimistic or optimistic, I say I'm neither. Because if you say you're optimistic, then presumably you don't have to do anything yourself about the problems because they'll take care of themselves. And if you say you're pessimistic, it's discouraging, because you've already adopted the foregone conclusion, which I haven't. I think that as long as there's life, there is hope. But there is so much destruction of life in every sphere – plants, trees, animals, human beings – that, as long as there is life, there's hope, for there must be some life left with which to hope.

Dubal: I'm always frustrated when people say, 'Oh, there will always be wars – it's human nature.' 'Well then,' I say, 'our conversation is over. It's stagnant. There can be no other way. War then must prevail – it's human nature.' South Africa is going to be one of the great testing grounds in the history of race relations.

Menuhin: That's a terrible, terrible situation. We're reaping the havoc of hundreds of years of abuse. And the people who enjoyed life in South Africa enjoyed a wonderful life. Blessed, wonderful nature, plenty of opportunity and scope for everything. But we have to pay – other generations have to pay the price of previous generations' indulgence.

When I was there first, in 1935 – now that's fifty-five years ago – we went down gold mines and also saw how the people lived in those days. The labour that came were actually separated from their village, from their township. For years they had no opportunity of going out of the compound. They got some pittance of wages with which they could buy perhaps a few bicycles when they were allowed to return. That was taken for granted, that was normal. Surely that's not normal; surely the people who gave of their lives and their toil, their sweat, to create the wealth of South Africa, surely they are entitled to that wealth, to a part of that

126

wealth, to the part they worked for. And that has never been
acknowledged. That excess wealth goes into arms to beat
them down. Now they're becoming more and more self-
conscious, now there is a whole ideology that they can adopt:
anti-church, anti Reformed Church, the Dutch church
which prevails there, the church that preached that God
willed it that there were white people who He made with
preference, and black people who He originally conceived to
belong to those, who were not considered of the sort of preferred species. And now they joined the anti-church. I mean,
it's rife and ripe for an equally dangerous doctrine, which
also is gradually being, how shall I say, retreated from in
Russia, as in China. I mean, I was very interested to read
Gorbachev's new concept, where he said, Communism is not
really for now – that we have to realize that we're neither
spiritually nor materially prepared for it. We have to realize
that capitalism is strong, though it's past its zenith, but it
is a realistic attitude. But those who are suffering, and for
those who are tortured, they need a doctrine which is totally
consoling of the hereafter; even if it's only in the next generation, even if it's only five years from now, it'll be paradise.
But they need something totally consoling. And they are
going to adopt this simply because we, I say *we*, the Western
world, perhaps we have, as the Eastern has in its own time,
whenever they have a chance, abused power. Whenever
people have an advantage, instead of ploughing it back and
turning it into a preparation for a better world, they exploit it
to the very full. There have been colossal mistakes. Look at
the whole mistake of the colonial system in changing the
vegetation of the islands to sugar cane. One of the worst
decisions ever taken. The sweet tooth – to favour the sweet
tooth, we were obliged to import African slaves, because no
one else would do that work in that heat. We were obliged to
massacre the local population of the Caribbean. We imported
this sugar because that was the most delicious thing we could

eat, and we have created famine and an unbalanced economy in a host of places, which should never have grown sugar cane in the first place. That is one of the colossal mistakes of history. And now we're paying the price.

Dubal: In today's world, religion seems more violent even than ever before.

Menuhin: It is an amazing phenomenon, this fanatical fundamentalism. We have seen certain revivalist movements. I think there was a rather strong fundamentalist movement in the South in the United States at one time.

Dubal: There still is, and the TV preachers are absolutely laughable, if they weren't so dangerous. What are your thoughts on Islam?

Menuhin: Islam has been torn apart for so long by its different tribes and different branches. Somehow or other in that Middle Eastern area – I don't know whether it's geographical or whether it's the desert – it breeds a kind of fanaticism, religious fanaticism. It breeds religion, for one thing. There is a very fine tract of Freud on monotheism and the desert. This tract of Freud on monotheism and the relation of monotheism to the desert. He seems to feel that the unity of the space, the simplicity of the desert, unbroken by trees or mountains or anything, led perhaps to the first thought of monotheism. Whereas in the countryside that is broken by many different shades of green, and many different types of vegetation and geographical sites, that perhaps people would be more diverse. Like the Greeks: the coastline of Greece itself, which is so full of little valleys and individual cultures that have sprung up specifically in various little regions, may have led to a diversity of gods. But the one thing about the Middle East is that this tribal relationship of one group of people to the other is so strong; both the loyalties within the tribe are immense, and the rivalries and the conflicts are also very great. It is a militant religion certainly, Mohammedanism. And yet if you read the Sufi books, at its highest it is as noble, as wise, as tolerant as the greatest religions of the world, as Judaism or Christianity or Buddhism. It is as philosophical. Some of my favourite readings are Sufi stories and anecdotes; they are absolutely unbelievable. So that it does *live* at the very height. But this is a kind of surrender, shall we say, again perhaps to frustration, and to the desire for recapturing a very great culture, a very great empire that extended at the time from Gibraltar to Indonesia, went through India and to Indonesia, of which now only remnants are left. Bali, by the way, is Hindu, it's not Mohammedan Indian. But this is an atavism, and somehow also a return to simplicity. The mental requirements for today's survival are such that the temptation of black and white, as in Germany (even this great country of Germany succumbed to black and white), the simplicity of saying this is good, this is bad. And we must understand too that we have given the Mohammedans, we have given Islam certainly valuable grounds for resentment. Whether this would have come about, whether Iran would have come about with or without the Shah, I don't know. But certainly things are worse in Iran now than they had ever been under the Shah. To be at the mercy of people who think they are infallible and who have absolute power is one of the curses of humanity. And we must never look upon a situation with a sense of superiority. I mean the fact that we are in no way comparable to Iran, that we are not under the leadership of an Ayatollah with extreme powers and the sense of the righteousness of the Koran, doesn't mean that we aren't in some degree in danger of this black and white mentality. It still is a dangerous temptation for people who are tired of having to weigh subtle differences and who are not prepared to do that, and don't have the time to do that, and want to get on and say, 'Well, give it to a dictator, let him decide. Let's

have order.' Well, the whole business of discussing order:
again, is order something you can impose or does it have to
grow, shouldn't it grow from within the person through
self-discipline, and so on. It's a very difficult ordeal when
you think of what these people have to suffer. We have gone
through hundreds of years of British history. From the
Magna Carta on down. And we have inherited that, we have
built our own laws in the same spirit. And there we see today
the rise, first in Hitler – already in Lenin – but now in *many*
dictators coming up, some of the most brutal, as Amin and
Bokasa; upstarts, with not even the Koran to draw upon.
And then someone who feels saintly and has the conviction
of righteousness and infallibility, like the Ayatollah, with
apparently no humility. These are modern dangers that are
on all sides threatening us, this mentality. I don't think we
are in danger of that kind of fundamentalism here. We are far
too advanced in the electronic, scientific, self-critical sense.
Because when you are dealing with studies in nature, there
is an element there that keeps you after all to a certain truth.
I mean, you cannot pretend any longer that the earth is flat,
for instance. You cannot pretend that there are less than so
and so many elements. You cannot pretend that there are
less than so and so many speeds. Therefore, you are dealing
already with relativity. We are beyond the point when we can
fall back, I think, into pure black and white. Because from
Einstein on, and presumably from before him, Galileo and
others, we have already embraced the relativity of everything
– of speeds, and of weights and of gravity and so on. But
before there was proof, before the world had proof of this
relativity, energy and mass, and believers and non-believers,
and nationals and aliens, they were black and white. And I
think Islam is precisely an example of a country and a people
that hadn't yet bridged that enormous gap between a society
that had everything determined by religious edict . . . as the
Jewish society was; in other words, when you bathe, how

you bathe, what you eat, how you rise, how you make love to your wife, everything was determined. I am talking of a theocracy. So that Iran never evolved sufficiently to shake off all that heritage of a theocracy, and Israel *has*. I don't think there is any danger of Israel being a theocracy.

Dubal: You once said that Israel will possibly now suffer from being a nationality.

Menuhin: Can it go beyond that? Well, I think there are very good signs: that demonstration in Jerusalem that drew – was it 500,000 people? – who were criticizing the Lebanon adventure. That, I think, is an indication of at least a very large body of opinion in Israel that's thinking not only of immediate self-defence – which is justified – but of ultimate co-operation. I think unless you keep that ideal in front of the people and repeat it every day, unless you say that what we want is to be people among our neighbours, and to give them the same feeling that we have achieved, and to treat them as equals – unless that is repeated every day, then the *other* will get the upper hand. This fear, which is justified, up to a point, it is justified; they are surrounded by enemies, but to a certain extent, they have contributed to this attitude. And to the extent that it is at all humanly possible to protect an ideal society, it should be done. The history of Jerusalem is one of the most tragic histories of any city in the world. Jerusalem has been sacked more often than any other city.

Dubal: Yes. It is a city of tears. If only we could have faith instead of beliefs . . .

Menuhin: Yes, we must have faith that someday Jerusalem will be regarded with equal veneration by all those who find their origins there, their religious origins, their holy past.

As for the Israelis, what will you do with people who, quite understandably, have looked to Jerusalem as their haven, their home, for thousands of years; finally have it, love it, respect it, make the most of it, and don't want to share that power over Jerusalem with anybody else? And the others, who . . . If only they found a few with whom they could share it, *that* would already be a beginning, or just the promise that eventually it would be . . . But they are quite right; I mean, no universal power can administer Jerusalem as well as it is administered today. The Arabs and the Jews can't do it together, because the Arabs who did it would be assassinated by their own people. The Jews can't do it, because it is difficult for them emotionally to share that holy, sacred place, and therefore it cannot happen today. But if only, I would already be grateful . . . For instance, when a bomb was thrown by a Jewish fanatic at an Arab bus the other day, I was in Jerusalem with Diana at the time, on a Sunday. And the President, who we met in the afternoon, came to the concert. This was just after this had happened, and we spoke about it. I said, 'But these were Israeli Arabs. They were assassinated by a Jewish fanatic. Here is an opportunity to declare a day of mourning in Jerusalem, just to show, to give an example of impartiality.' Of course, they never did it. But I feel that probably they couldn't have done it. Maybe the President would have been assassinated. I just don't know.

Dubal: Did you ever think that your friend Indira Gandhi would be killed by a terrorist religious group?

Menuhin: No. But then, look at what happened to Gandhi himself. And everybody has firearms today. The capacity, the ability to annihilate today is greater than ever, not only on a grand scale, but on a small scale. Everybody owns guns. There are manuals on how to destroy authority and governments. There are manuals on how to make revolutions; there are manuals on how to make homemade bombs, and there are schools. Guerrillas are being taught in international schools today.

Dubal: How can the terrorist situation be fought?

Menuhin: We cannot answer them with the same treatment. We must absolutely push our defences as far as possible, but we must leave doors open for redemption, for even the guerrillas. Because, after all, Begin was a guerrilla in his day, and he has become quite respectable.

Dubal: But I am also frightened of respectability.

Menuhin: Oh, yes, that's true. But nonetheless, the element of fighting outside the confines of the establishment, of the established state, is something that has spurred the imagination of many people. We have had a tradition in the United States, a very great tradition of lawlessness.

Dubal: As well as Thoreau's *Civil Disobedience*.

Menuhin: Yes, absolutely. So we admire that underneath in some of our accepted respectabilities.

Dubal: You seem to be that Zen ideal where the world is moving around you, and you're understanding every aspect of what's going on. And yet there is a feeling of calm and peace.

Menuhin: Well, it's misleading, you know. I am no better than anybody else when it comes to worrying about people, about family. If my wife isn't well or I expect her back and she isn't or anything like that happens, I am just as anxious as any other person would be.

Dubal: Have you read a book called *Zen and the Art of Archery?*

Menuhin: Yes indeed, I think it's a wonderful book. And actually we do practise it, up to a point, in violin playing. Because we don't actually see the spots that we have to hit, and we try to be as accurate as possible. But of course it's different with an arrow, shooting it at a distance. There, every slightest angle would alter the bull's-eye. So that's much more exacting. We don't have to throw our fingers from that distance on to the fingerboard and hope they don't miss.

Dubal: You've said the human race is prone to blame, but the violinists, the instrumentalists on stage, can blame nobody but themselves.

Menuhin: That is the good thing about a musician that he must learn and he can't avoid learning; that if he plays a note out of tune, no one else has played it. Maybe he can say the string is defective, that is a possibility. But then he changes the string, and if the note is still out of tune, he can't say that any longer. It's very useful, I think, and I wish that some such experience of really direct responsibility would be more generally accepted. A small example: on the Concorde the other day we were late, and the last quarter of an hour was spent standing in that corridor, that rather narrow corridor in the Concorde, waiting to disembark while the plane was finding its gate. Finally the captain rang and said, 'It's entirely my fault.' I thought that was rather nice.

Dubal: Sociologically – what do you most fear?

Menuhin: I hate the mob, I hate any kind of mob. I know how easily it can be twisted – a promise, a scapegoat, an assurance of superiority. That's all they need – something to give them a feeling of worth.

Dubal: In Nazi Germany, Hitler won his way through the manipulation of the deprived lower middle class. Hitler made them into a raving mob.

Menuhin: People aren't educated to look at themselves and blame themselves first. In any situation when people are upset, they immediately want to find whose fault it is, who is guilty. Not our own, if possible. If Hitler had managed to find some other scapegoat, or to use the Jews, but to have been less total in their annihilation, he would have had them working for him in Germany. Absolutely – they were as good and loyal and patriotic Germans as you could hope to have. And then when you think of behaviour, it's long past the moment when we could single the Germans out as the only horrible people. Look what Stalin did. Look what China has done, Vietnam, look what the Israelis are now doing. Do you know that during World War II, the United States turned back a shipload of Jews and sent them back to Germany?

Dubal: Absolutely did, and Roosevelt knew about it, nor was Churchill lily white in the matter of the Jews.

Menuhin: This business of blaming others must stop – I think we have to learn to forget – I think we must forget – and to turn our minds to the common purposes which are so pressing, whether it's education, whether it's pollution, drugs, whether it's a sense of values, an order of values, whether it's protecting the young and their future, whether it's the cleansing of our society or our minds. And we can't cure anything with brutal aims. We have to do it from a positive angle. There is so much that must be done, and we can only start doing it if we forget the past. As long as we are going to keep up ancient feuds – our parents were murdered, and until we murder your parents things can't be straight. You know the old Sicilian Family, everybody is seeking revenge and piling it on so there is more and more of an accumulation of a commitment to revenge.

Dubal: Presently the world is talking about German unification, something which nobody thought would be possible only an hour ago, so to speak.

Menuhin: Yes, this is of the highest interest to the world. I'd like to read a letter I wrote to the London *Times* which was published about this subject and its ramifications:

Sir, I pray that in the present deliberation on a United Germany's loyalties and allegiances we will not find ourselves debating two equally unrealistic alternatives – viz, Nato versus neutrality – while, in fact, an independent, strong Germany is deciding for herself.

Germany belongs to a European Community, and the United Germanies together should belong to a United Joint East and West European Community – an alliance yet to be achieved.

To covet East Germany for Nato smacks too much of former discredited camp coalitions and pacts, political solutions which created, three times since 1870, the climate for German aggression and war. To suggest that a great European power should be neutral, especially when the eastern and western parts already adhere to two different consignments, is unrealistic.

Might, therefore, a suspension of a United Germany's military commitments, until such moment when political pressures will have achieved a United Europe – in de Gaulle's prophetic words, 'from the Channel to the Urals' – not be the wisest course to follow?

When, in the ripeness of time, this enlarged European Community will happen (and with the fluidity of present events it is not too sanguine to anticipate that necessary combination of good will and common sense from all quarters which could hasten the development), a federated Germany, along with all the other semi-autonomous regions, would embrace the collective obligations of the community, i.e. –

1. To defend and keep the peace,

2. To provide an example of the federative process to areas whose problems can only be solved along these lines.

3. To plan to live within our resources and not beyond them, conserving and renewing air, water, earth, energy, food, and life with dignity, vigilance, and harmony.

Dubal: What about China?

Menuhin: The proper answer for China is not to prepare for defeat. The answer to China today is to join all those countries who still believe in some sort of dignity of man, collectively against the menace which China might become if it remains a tyranny for another ten years.

Dubal: Did you think that the events of 1989 with the students would happen?

Menuhin: No, I didn't – I still had some hope.

Dubal: Hope is the greatest cheat of all. We can't live in hope. It keeps us waiting.

Menuhin: Absolutely! Absolutely. It was all a near-miss. They were certainly divided in the upper echelon in China. If they now create a Nazi state – because that's what it is. China now is the first instance of a Fascist-Communist synthesis. It's Fascist in the sense that it wants all the commerce with the West and the industry and the development of material wealth. But it wants control at the same time. Well, you can't have it ultimately, you can't have both together.

Dubal: So this is a great moment in the history of evil. China now takes the spotlight.

Menuhin: Exactly! There has never been as clear a juxtaposition – a crystallization of good and evil – as today. It's most focused. It's really good and evil. In the United States, we live still a rather comfortable admixture of good and evil. It's so inherent in whatever our atomic nucleus is. We know that evil is equatable with good, and a little good in every evil.

Dubal: Or the truth in the false, and the false in the truth.

Menuhin: Yes, and that, I think, is a fairly tolerable human condition. But there are certain pressures, like the pressure that creates new materials and new chemicals and so on. That now is creating nearly unadulterated evil, such as the terrorists, and nearly unadulterated good, like those students in China with their Statue of Liberty. It's a fascinating and terrifying time when we have these two elements in their relatively pure state. Because that is what this present world is about. Until now we had materials which contained everything. The material of life: the living cell, the material of rock and so on. And then human ingenuity tried to find the pure material in everything. The elements. And the same with human emotions. We once had a nice admixture. Now we've come to the point where we can isolate pleasure in the brain, and give the pleasure of the sensation only by putting an electrode in the right place – can't we? And so we have a monkey living in sheer delight – doesn't know what it's about. But he's so happy because he has an electrode in the right place, and no doubt other places that can be used for torture, which create pain, misery and depression. And specialization, which is another form of isolation. Now we're seeking integration in groups and think-tanks, in dentists who know something about music. We are seeking a renewal of integration. But good and evil are now in certain places, as this confrontation in China was as near as one can get to good and evil balancing each other out. The Four Horses of the Apocalypse are upon us now. Very shortly – already in terms of famine. We are not prepared against famine, as the Incas were. The topsoil in the United States is reduced to only a few inches now.

Dubal: With a drought in the Midwest, there can be another dust bowl.

Menuhin: There can be another easily. After the last Ice Age, apparently the topsoil was tens of feet deep. It's been a natural evolution, but very much hastened by forms of cultivation, by deforestation. So we need another Ice Age. However, there are new elements that are altering the natural cycle, as we are consuming our resources, completely and destroying the ozone. The winds are getting faster. There

again we have an example of polarization – good and evil –
the extreme winds. In politics the centre which is balanced is
giving way to extremes in certain places. You try hard to
keep the middle, but nonetheless it's being torn apart. In
Israel, the Middle East, it's being torn apart – there are still
many who want to keep the middle road, but it's getting
rather difficult. In terms of natural things winds are getting faster and slower, temperatures are getting hotter and
colder. Fanaticisms are running at higher temperature than
before.

Dubal: And what of Russia – a people you love – we could
spend hours in discussion.

Menuhin: The Russians must give the people something.
They are disorganized. There is no distribution of goods,
there is no incentive to produce anything. These poor Russians
who are mystics and who have to have a great vision. They
are people who follow a vision. They are sacrificed for a vision,
because life is so terrible – as Diana says, buried in either
mud or snow; in winter it's snow, in summer it's mud – and
having absolutely nothing to live for. So they live for what
they can produce on the stage and in their imagination. Literary people on an unprecedented level, singing people, love
for poetry, musical, always ready for self-sacrifice. Of course,
the Russians may change as they embrace our values, as they
more and more imitate us. They may be quite different in
only a very few years.

Dubal: Quite different – as the Japanese have changed drastic-
ally, with, as Susan Sontag says, the miracle of the inflated
yen.

Menuhin: Of course, the Japanese were always working
people; they were people who knew how to economize. The
Russians have to spend themselves to the point of self-
sacrifice. They have an enormous country, and nothing is too

big for them. Everything goes to infinity. Their thoughts go to infinity. Their eyes dwell upon infinity. What is close to them is so sad and so poor, so distressing. The Japanese are tight insular people, and make the most of very little, and know how to work very hard, and are digitally gifted because they work with chopsticks to start with. Their eyes and minds and fingers are precise; they can do little things perfectly; they can miniaturize. The Russians can only handle big blocks of granite. The Russians are clumsy by comparison, although they make marvellous dancers and acrobats.

Dubal: Do you feel we are gradually losing touch with music stemming from the human voice as if it all springs from the keyboard or electronic instruments?

Menuhin: Yes. Now, of course, with these synthetic sounds and the electronic sounds, we can put it on to tape without the middleman, without the interpreter, without the performer. It's interesting. I have nothing against these experiments. I think they are useful and in their way important to explore. Because our age differs from any other age, in that we don't see black and white, we begin to see by degrees. There's a degree between noise and meaningful noise and music, between organized sound, collages of sound, as we have collages for pictures. This experimentation into degrees I'm not at all averse to, because I think it renders us a little more subtle in our understanding that between the guerrilla and the policeman, between the bad man and the good man, there are many stages and degrees. So that we have something in common that may make it possible one day for us to be on speaking terms and, as I say, redeem.

Dubal: Goliath may not have been such a monster totally, and we know that even Hitler painted watercolours.

Menuhin: Yes, whether Hitler was redeemable, I doubt it.

Dubal: You're right, he was beyond redemption, and Stalin was absolutely insane. How does it happen that these very few are followed by the many?

Menuhin: Because the many, by definition, can only follow a madman.

Dubal: That's the most depressing of all comments though.

Menuhin: Not at all. If they are really frustrated and they are miserable, it's only a madman who would understand them and who could promise them the things that no sensible man would promise them; who would tell them things to build up their ego, their pride; who would say, 'It's all these Jews' or 'It's all these Pakistanis' or 'It's all these Blacks or Catholics, Irish, Protestants' – we've always had that. Jews are by no means singled out to be the only persecuted race in the world. What about the Armenians? In fact, there again I think the Jews naturally were taken up with their own suffering. But when they created a stage, and when money came from Germany – which I wasn't in favour of, I don't think you can buy off a crime like that. The fact that you can pay that much and then wash your hands – not that the Germans have washed their hands, they haven't. They're very good about it. They're the most civilized nation in the world today because they are expiating a crime, and you have to have a measure of guilt to be civilized.

Dubal: What are your thoughts about anti-Semitism and its tradition?

Menuhin: Once anti-Semitism is accepted practice, it makes the practitioner innocent. It becomes normal behaviour, accredited and sanctioned by tradition. The Jews cannot simply condemn the Polish, Russian and German people. You have to condemn the tradition. And now that there are almost no Jews in Poland or Germany the tradition is changing.

They are different now; they are becoming different. You see, if the Jews in Israel and elsewhere had worried about *all* those who were victims of Fascism and Communism and not only the Jews, it would have made a very, very great difference.

Dubal: Yes, in Paris recently I saw a memorial on some side street to the fallen Jews. It's now guarded by the police from terrorists.

Menuhin: If that had been a memorial to those fallen at the hands of the Nazis – Jews, gypsies, Eastern races, lower races – to a false mentality, that wouldn't have to be guarded by the police. That's where we've gone wrong.

Dubal: Let's speak on what is a tumultuous problem along with beer and vulgarity generally – *noise*. No country in the world has more noise than the United States.

Menuhin: Oh, I couldn't agree with you more. I brought this matter up with Unesco once, asking if we couldn't encourage some general aspect, some general measures to be taken, not only to reduce pollution of noise, but to institute quiet periods, silence. I mean, silence used to be part of every religious service, of meditation, too. In fact at my school, every morning when they meet and sing and are given a good thought, whether poetical, philosophical, whatever it may be, religious, mystic, it's followed by two minutes, approximately, of silence. Silence is one of the most precious commodities.

Dubal: There's two good books by Murray Schafer, the Canadian composer, *The Soundscape* and *The Tuning of the World*, on sound and noise.

Menuhin: Aren't they excellent? He has specialized in creating and discovering and researching what he calls the 'soundscape'. Instead of the visual landscape, he reproduces the aural environment as it existed in different epochs in different places, which was totally different from ours. I mean the smithy hammering away at the horseshoes, the carriages going on cobbles, and of course no electric motors. We have a constant basic ground tone, an organ point almost everywhere, of electric motors, which are inescapable. What Schafer calls 'noise with no signal value'. In other words, let's say for primitive people or for the Red Indian, if he took a walk in the country, every noise he heard had significance. In other words, if a leaf rustled, it was some animal going or a man or some particular wind that was blowing from a particular direction, because it was that particular sound that particular kind of leaf made. And if it was a bird call, it meant something to him; he could probably understand whether it was a call of warning or of fear or of delight or whatever it may have been. Today we are surrounded with sound which is meaningless.

Dubal: Yes, and I don't agree with John Cage that all noise is equal.

Menuhin: No, I don't at all either. But we have this noise without signal value, and that is an encumbrance on our existence. To be surrounded with meaninglessness is one aspect of noise, as great a nuisance as the volume that renders us deaf. Between the two I wouldn't know which to choose, the fact that it's meaningless or the fact that it's intolerable. Both are horrible. And we deaden our senses, we become numb. We become numb to pain – our own – and by extension, we become numb to other people's pain too.

Dubal: The numbing prodigality of the violence that we see on television, the noise we hear, we're becoming numb. And that's the great danger of this.

Menuhin: Yes, I cannot understand those people who say that they don't believe that television has any influence on us. It's such nonsense. *Everything* has an influence on us. If one talks to a human being, it's an influence, surely. We learn. If one breathes air, it's an influence for good or bad. You cannot pretend that something that takes hours of each day . . .

Dubal: Seven and a half hours of every American's day is spent watching TV.

Menuhin: Unbelievable. You cannot pretend that seven and a half hours are spent on something that leaves no trace whatsoever, it's nonsense.

Dubal: Of course it's nonsense. Why would there be 400 million hand guns in the United States? It seems eight out of ten scenes on television have a gun in them. Chekhov once said that if in Act I there is a gun on the desk, it has to be used in the play.

Menuhin: Of course. And then seen by children on television, and seeing the same character come back the next week after he's been shot dead, they have no idea of what it means.

Dubal: All of this produces numbing and a feeling of helplessness. Just as you think you have discovered a lake so far from the crowd, a whole brigade of motor boats will roar through the silence. The motor is inescapable.

Menuhin: And the pure silence of those snowscapes in Canada has been largely ruined by these snowmobiles. The most hideous noise I know is the sound of the electric tree cutter. I think that's hideous; I can't bear it.

Dubal: Air pollution is hideous, but nothing is psychologically as harmful to all of us as this unbelievably meaningless noise. How can a city like New York have a subway system so ghastly? It's like descending into hell. And people begin to look hellish.

Menuhin: You know, I had plans for New York during the war, when it was really the greatest city in the world, the most wonderful city in the world. My plans were relatively simple, but they would need a little effort. They consisted in three different measures. One was to clear out three or four floors from every building, the bottom of every building, so that you'd have free pedestrian motion throughout the block. Instead of the pedestrian being squeezed between the road and the building, he'd just walk through the building underneath. In fact, all the apartment houses in Tel Aviv are built on that principle. It would be quite easy. You'd leave, of course, the lift shaft, the elevator shaft, but otherwise, it would be cleared. That would be one thing. Then you'd build over the present streets garden streets so that all the streets would be planted with trees. The present roadway would be maintained, but only for electric transport. So that you'd look down on quiet, green squares, nothing but green and electric transport below. Then the other thing was a sort of catwalk, covered, between all the buildings that were above a certain level, at an average level so that you'd have entrances to those buildings from a high level as well as from street level. Which would mean that you could do your shopping promenading between buildings at a certain height, say an average of whatever it is – twenty storeys or fifteen or whatever – and go into the building from that level, taking the pressure away from the street level. That kind of imaginative job could have been done.

And of course, subways are a disgrace. There is so much money in New York, but all of it private, none of it is available for public works. One of the propaganda measures that Russians could do is not to send money and food to the British miners, who really don't need it – nobody starves in England – but give New York a new subway system. Wouldn't that be a tremendous gesture?

Dubal: That would be one of the great gestures in human history.

Menuhin: And not likely to happen. But I think that any society, to be stable, must have a basic level below which people can't sink. After that, let them compete as much as they like. The strength of Italy used to be that it had cheap pasta and cheap oranges. That meant that no one need go hungry, they'd have that. Now everything is so geared to price that nothing good is cheap; things that are cheap are generally poisonous. For instance, England during the war at least had good bread, and health was never better. As a minimum, a country must have a good loaf, fruit in season, tents for shelter, if need be a winter coat, a good pair of shoes – those kind of things should be free, totally free. And then let people compete as much as they want to for everything else.

Dubal: Absolutely. Why don't governments put your plans to use?

Menuhin: My plans have never been put to use. But I just feel a little better for five minutes when I speak about them. But I have no illusions.

Dubal: Cities are out of touch with people – urban life has lost its former ability to bring stimulation.

Menuhin: Yes, what I feel is it's a great mistake in any city to build office blocks and office districts. Every district should be lived in. The buildings should go up that are part office and part residential, so that people needn't commute. So that people can live near their work, as in the old days, the crafts-men and their families. And today, even the few people who make shoes by hand do them at home; they live with their family. Many people I know pursue their craft, whether it's making violins, in their home. Why do cities become derelict, devastated areas at night when the offices are closed? Because the people assume they have to live elsewhere. Why? Wall Street would be a wonderful place to live in if half the space were for apartments and dwelling places, theatres and all the rest – how exciting to live there.

Dubal: Yes. We have to have a drastic relook at the way we live in cities.

Menuhin: New York is better off than other cities, because at least people live in Madison Avenue and work down on the streets, but other cities are totally dead at night.

Dubal: Yes, totally dead and, of course, based on fear.

Menuhin: Yes. Another thing – architects. Buildings should never be only office buildings but also dwellings. Again, a little village in the Middle Ages or more recently used to have its Town Hall and used to have its library and so on. Why isn't it obligatory on any building that houses more than so and so many hundreds of people, that they have a place where amateur sculptors can work, where musicians can practise, where people can get together for a lecture? It should be part and parcel of every group of a few hundred people. Now you have the monstrosity of cities of fourteen million with less cultural facilities than would be normal in a city of 300,000. What happens is that those cultural facilities that exist are of a very high order. I mean, the Metropolitan Opera is superb, the concerts you get there, that's superb. The quality and the pressure of a big city produces standards that are unbeatable. But one cannot sacrifice millions and millions of people to standards only. There must be high standards, but there must be a compromise whereby the millions of people have also something, some culture and some opportunities in their lives. Now, what we are discussing is basic. I think, an edict, a law whereby no building or co-op is without communal rooms in it for various purposes – artistic, intellectual, whatever it may be.

Dubal: Or a whole room just to come and practise yoga in.

Menuhin: Also gymnasiums, and yoga, and meditation.

Dubal: Meditation and yoga became an important part of your life after you discovered India.

Menuhin: Yes, indeed. I never really did Indian meditation. I meditate in my music when I study a score or when I think about it. But I use the Hatha Yoga, which is the postures, breathing also; breathing is a very important aspect of yoga. The sad thing in our life, which is the civilized life, is that by definition civilization is the taking away of what is natural and supplanting of it by what is man-made – art, if you wish, or a craft. People have to learn to breathe; they have to learn to walk; they have to learn to be natural. They have to learn everything, and very few people have the chance to do that.

Dubal: I think language has never been more debased and people, especially the young, don't trust language anymore.

Menuhin: Yes, and look at the words that have been debased. I mean, you can't use the word 'peace' without talking politics. You can't use the word 'freedom' any longer; no one knows what it means. People think it's licence. It's quite terrifying. And yet the causes of the evil are so obvious: lack of home, lack of love, lack of cohesion – social cohesion – noise, all the pesticides, all the poisons. We are absorbing poisons at a rate that is devastating. They have proven that lead in the water from old lead pipes in Liverpool leads to insanity. It's proven on monkeys. Do you know that the bleaching agent that has been used in white bread since 1870, when they introduced those first white bread metals – what do you call them – that took all the bran and the wheat germ out of the flour – mills, the metal milling process – then they used an agent to bleach the flour, which they've only stopped about twenty years ago. During fifty or sixty years, the American people were fed bread with a bleaching agent that made monkeys go mad. So it isn't any wonder.

Dubal: Well, food is another subject – what *junk food* has done to the human body, you can see all over America in the enormously overweight people. Europeans coming to the US are always astounded by how many fat Americans there are.

Torture and political murder has been revived in our brutal times. By the end of the nineteenth century, it was an ideal of the so-called civilized world, at least not to torture people anymore.

Menuhin: We thought that was the Middle Ages. Now it's back in full swing.

Dubal: Everywhere from Uganda to Argentina, to Iran and Central America, there are torture chambers.

Menuhin: It's become an international – how shall I say? – craft. They exchange information; they document it; there are machines built, there are electric gadgets built. It's an industry; it has a vested interest of its own. The most important thing that could be done would be to document the names of every one of these people so that they would know that they would be brought to trial.

Dubal: Think of your former accompanist, when they found out he was a Jew, the pianist; the fingers would be broken instantly – think of such gangsterism. We have it world-wide again, the brutality of this century.

Menuhin: Yes. And then we have television. And because the commercial world must cater to the lowest common denominator, we have therefore nothing but sex and violence. Violence is the quickest form of assertiveness. If you can't construct, you destroy, and you destroy quickly and then you are famous for it. So the most loathsome human characteristics – brutal, violent, disloyal, distrustful – these are coming to the fore, because they are commercially viable. Or they are viable in a state like Russia, where violence is state violence. So that in a way they have it under control; they have absorbed it into the state, and the state does the violence, and no one else is allowed to do it. But one thing you cannot have its state drunkenness. That really is common to all the Russians. That's a great problem in Russia. It's a problem here too.

Dubal: Is Switzerland a civilized nation – the best-run country on earth?

Menuhin: Yes, Switzerland is unbelievably civilized. It's the best-run little country in the world.

Dubal: Maybe the word here is 'little'; it has to all be little to work.

Menuhin: Maybe – maybe it has to be little. It's interesting no one knows the name of the President, who is elected once a year for a year, in rotation, between a German, French and Italian. There is never a woman, however.

Dubal: Finally the Swiss women are now able to vote.

Menuhin: Yes. They're very conservative. But the President travels by streetcar and no one gets up when he enters the streetcar. And there's no show of military. Everyone owns a gun and he never misuses a gun. You never hear of a Swiss going berserk and using his gun in the wrong way.

Dubal: Let me read some lines by Clive Bell from a book titled *Civilization* written in 1928 – five years before Hitler came into official power.

> What is called a man or a woman of action is almost always a deformed and deficient artist who yearns to express himself or herself but, unable to express by creating, must assert by interfering. These are the people who need power, who cannot live by thought and feeling. These are the makers of war and empires, and the troublers of peace.

Menuhin: Well, Mr Bell has certainly a strong point there. Men of action. I know very many of our epithets, very many of our ideas, still come from the cave age when you had to have a certain brute power. Although, for all I know, the caveman needn't have been any more brutal than some of the people living today; and at least I don't imagine he was more brutal than some of the animals that needed what they had to have for survival. I've always been dubious about men of action.

Dubal: Mr Bell continues:

> What is peculiar to civilized people is, in the first place, that they are capable of recognizing the value of knowledge as a means to exquisite spiritual states. And in the second place, that they esteem this value above any remote utilitarian virtue.

Menuhin: That's interesting. There's certainly the spiritual element, the symbolic element that's essential. It can often also take a wrong turn. Because when we divorce ourselves too much from reality, we then contrive another reality, which may be a wrong reality. There's nothing that stops the human mind from espousing every kind of aberration. Look at the Germans, with their gift for abstraction and philosophy, in their worst moments they produced yielded Hitler.

Dubal: Yes, with all their might, they gave their souls to Hitler, a failed artist. Then Germans gave up their conscience, the very soul that created Dürer and Bach to Kant and Marx.

Menuhin: Yes. Which just shows that there's no knife that can't be turned against the bearer.

Dubal: George Steiner said that 'an imagination too utterly absorbed and fascinated by great art and literature can become autistic. The cry in the streets seems mysteriously less powerful, less important, than the cry in the book, or in the story.' And so many people are addicted to art in the worst way now.

Menuhin: Yes. I think one can understand Mao, who's now been debunked from his hero status for sending his artists to the countryside, making them work on the farms. Or the Russian desire for art that is for the people, so they can sing and dance too. The fear of abstraction is an understandable one, although again, like anything else, *everything* pushed too far becomes an evil. That's why democracy can be wonderful, in which one side balances the other, and that's why a wife is wonderful; if she can call her husband back from his aberrations: 'What are you doing there?' to shrink him down to reality.

Dubal: Of the two sexes, which one lives more by aberration and unreality?

Menuhin: Oh, man does – woman much less. Women really have to produce and to live and to nurture and to protect and to succour.

Dubal: The man can go off to war, to Congress or Parliament, but the woman will take care of the child until it grows up.

Menuhin: Yes, and the man is the dangerous animal because he lives by his visions. He would like to achieve this or that. Sometimes his achievements are noble, sometimes they are great. But sometimes they are sheer perversity. He is a very, very dangerous animal, man, and largely uncontrollable, and now bent apparently on self-destruction. And yet mankind has had many grand ideals.

Dubal: What is a worthwhile ideal?

Menuhin: Well, I would say a worthwhile ideal is one that protects life rather than finds a scapegoat and attacks life. I would say the young people who go out in a boat to defend a whale are to my mind absolutely pure, clean, laudable, courageous, and embody the best qualities in manhood and in human beings.

Dubal: And the whales are wonderful musicians and harmless.

Menuhin: Exactly. And we shall soon be faced with insoluble problems. Because if I put one such in front of you, who is to be Solomon and give us the answer? What is more worthwhile, to save the last twelve whales or 100,000 people somewhere? That is a very difficult problem to . . . It's not automatic, the answer isn't automatic by any means, because we are wasting people by the millions anyway. We are wasting them in famine, in cholera, in routine, in mental madness, in cancer. Conditions are terrible. We're wasting human beings. Are those human beings that are being wasted anyway and destroyed, are they worth twelve healthy whales? I don't know.

Dubal: What would be some of the qualities you would find necessary in a civilization?

Menuhin: Well, a civilization would have to have its own particular style of music and art. It would have to have its own beliefs and sacred values. Values, in other words, that were untouchable, that we couldn't change and must not be defiled. Hopefully, they would be living values attached to, not only to human life, but other life as well. And it would probably have some reflections of continuity, a sense of reverence, creativeness, order, social order, relation to neighbours.

Dubal: And what of organized religion?

Menuhin: I feel that the old, great religions need not be taken literally. What they inspire and what people found in them can still come from them provided we look upon them symbolically. We don't have to necessarily believe that our souls only arrive with baptism. Or that the Virgin Mary gave birth to Jesus. So many of our inherited thoughts become lost in the myths of time, and the Catholic Church has many beliefs which were pre-Catholic. This is true with the intermediary between our lives and God's – Jesus, who was nailed to the cross. But that has been the case with quite a few civilizations whose gods were torn apart by men or the beasts, who were sacrificed, or sacrificed themselves. There were parallels to Jesus, and therefore we should be able to take these ideas symbolically. And they can give us the same inspiration. But we live in a day of questioning, and the church has been hurt by rigid dogma.

Dubal: I was in a taxi and a religion salesman was on the radio taking questions from the phone, and one woman asked, 'How come God lets these earthquakes happen and all of this? If He cared about us, He wouldn't do that.' And the host, 'No, no, God has cursed us, and we're very lucky that he doesn't throw earthquakes at us every day. You should be grateful for that.' And this goes on the radio and TV day and night throughout the United States.

In fact, wherever one goes, one encounters religious fanatics. On the bus someone turned to me and said, 'You know, I'm going to go to heaven.' And I said, 'Well, when did you start believing that you would be going to heaven?' He said, 'I've been "born again" – and without believing in Jesus I wouldn't go to heaven. I have to believe now. I *will* believe; I don't want Satan to get me.' And he continued, 'Did you know that Jesus is God's only begotten Son?' I said something that stunned him: 'Well, you know, I'm surprised that God could only produce one Son, and no Daughters. I think he should have done much better.' He stopped for a minute, and said, 'Only one Son! I have two!'

Menuhin: Yes, it's incredible! We are seeing more and more extreme forms of belief, some very naïve. The simple answer to that is we were given a measure of self-determination, and we are expected to exercise that. We cannot hold God responsible for everything, neither for the miseries we bring upon ourselves, nor for the natural disasters, because it is not an anthropomorphic commander who is standing there with his computer mind on everything that goes on, and saying this shall happen to this person and that. There is, however, a fate; we are not only manufacturing, making our own world, but we are making a form of destiny of our own. We are contributing to it by our behaviour. Eventually, civilizations perish, not only because they are overthrown from outside or from within, but because of the weaknesses they have. And it can be a very small weakness, but it can accumulate. And there are always forces, beasts, whatever they may be, who are there to take advantage of every weakness. Like a scar, like a little cut, which one day will heal perfectly well, and another day, if we're not well, strong, or in good condition, it might fester. And thus we have quite a few weaknesses, and there are already on the horizon many forces that are trying to make the most of our weaknesses.

Dubal: Goethe once said to Eckermann: 'The world is not to be allowed to reach its goal as early as we think and hope. The retarding daemons are always there, interposing and opposing everywhere. Just you go on living, and you will see that I am right.'

How do you think of animals, whom we share this planet with?

Menuhin: I, for one, always feel that denying souls to animals is a great mistake. And we should know better than that today. 'Soul' is a curious word. It is very difficult to define. Everything is conscious in some degree – I think that we could admit. As Einstein believed that matter and energy have some relation between them, I think again we cannot believe that there are two totally unattached elements, life and matter. I think there must be some urge to life in the rawest bit of matter. I can't but believe there must be something inherent in the atom, which is mysterious or anything else. Even a living cell wants to belong; it wants to be part of something bigger. It has its function: surviving at the expense of something else or together with something else. It has, therefore, a certain consciousness. I think that there must be some consciousness even in the reaction of a split atom. It is interesting that many scientists are more mystical than other people who shop at the grocery store and think milk comes in cans.

Dubal: Humans have been endlessly cruel to animals. I know you have also been hurt about the treatment of the Red Indian.

Menuhin: Let me read you a most amazing letter from an Indian chief, Seathl, to Franklin Pierce, the President of the United States, in 1855, a document that combines the tragedy of the animal and the Indians:

> There is no quiet place in the white man's cities. No place to hear the leaves of autumn or the rustle of insects' wings. Perhaps because I am a savage and do not understand, the clatter insults the ears. And what is life if a man cannot hear the lovely call of the whippoorwill, or the argument of frogs around a pond at night? The Indian prefers the soft sound of the wind darting over the face of the pond; and the smell of the wind itself, cleansed by a mid-day rain or scented with pine. The air is precious to the red man, because all share the same breath – the beasts, the trees, and man himself. The white man does not seem to notice the air he breathes. Like a man dying for many days, he is numb to the smell of his own stench.

If I decide to accept [here Chief Seathl refers to land which the white man would like to buy], I will make one condition: the white man must treat the beasts of this land as his own brothers. I am a savage and do not understand any other way. I have seen a thousand rotting buffaloes on the prairies, left by the white man who shot them from a passing train. I am a savage and do not understand how the smoking iron horse can be more important than the buffalo that we kill only to live. What is man without the beast? If all the beasts were gone, man would die from great loneliness of spirit, for whatever happens to the beast also happens to man. All things are connected. Whatever befalls the earth befalls the sons of the earth.

Our children have seen their fathers humbled in defeat. Our warriors have felt shame. After defeat they spend their days in idleness, and contaminate their bodies with sweet foods and strong drink. It matters little where we pass the rest of our days – they are not many. A few more hours, a few more winters, and none of the children of the great tribes that once lived on this earth, or that roamed in small bands in the woods, will be left to mourn the graves of people once as powerful and hopeful as yours.

One thing we know, and the white man may one day discover the truth of it: our God is the same as your God. You may now think that you own Him in the same way that you wish to own our land. But you cannot. He is the God of man. And His compassion is equal for the red man and the white. This earth is precious to Him, and to harm the earth is to heap contempt upon its creator.

The whites too shall pass – perhaps sooner than other tribes. Continue to contaminate your bed and you will one night suffocate in your own waste. When the buffalo are all slaughtered, the wild horses all tamed, the secret corners of the forest heavy with the scent of many men, and the view of the ripe hills blotted by talking wives, where is the thicket? Gone. Where is the eagle? This marks the end of living and the beginning of survival.

We might understand if we knew what the white man

dreams, what hopes he describes to his children on long winter nights, what visions he burns into their minds so that they will wish for tomorrow. But we are savages. The white man's dreams are hidden from us. And because they are hidden, we will go our own way.

If we agree to sell our land, it will be to secure the Indian reservation you have promised us. There, perhaps, we may live out our brief days as we wish.

When the last red man has vanished from the earth, and the memory of him is like the shadow of a cloud moving across the prairie, these shores and forests will still hold the spirits of my people, for we love the earth as the newborn loves his mother's heartbeat.

Dubal: Today we have a world on the brink of new ideals. Europe is in a state of shock: not since 1848 has there been such complex commotion. But ideals scare me.

Menuhin: Oh yes, indeed! Communism was a great ideal. But in the hands of people who feel that they are called upon by destiny to create the great realization of an ideal, they don't stop at anything, it ends up with power, control, power-craze. I remember reading an interesting book by a doctor on human types. He says there are three human types, and various combinations of them. It depends upon the propensity of the body; we have the guts and the intestines, and those people who have that as preponderant drive, they have to feed their guts. And there is the digestive system. While the other is the muscular system, those are the drivers, the workers, the fighters. And there is the nervous system: those are the thinkers, the neurotics, and the intellectuals. And each have their type of extremists, and evil. The digestive system leads to greed. Any number of terribly fat people eating what the advertisements tell them to eat, horrible food, which adds nothing to their brain, their muscle or their nerve translated into political terms. It's partly the capitalist drive, the territorial desire.

Dubal: Yes, the quest for the 'more' – blessed be nothing, then nothing can own you.

Menuhin: That's a wonderful phrase. Yes, 'the more'. In the Arab world, more wives, no limit – that's the gut and intestine drive, the digestive drive. Then you have the muscular one translated into other terms. The extremist of this type has to control – has to have power, and domination. Of course, you have to control your muscles to play the violin; but the extremist of control is not interested in control of the muscles to play an instrument, they want to control everything within reach – the world if possible. And any dissenting voice is a flaw in the imperfect control. So you censor, you kill, you gag, you bind – anything – any dissenting voice is intolerable.

Dubal: Yes, not having total control is greatly painful to the authoritarian tyrant. And it's hard work.

Menuhin: It sure is hard work!

Dubal: This muscular thing is also translated into the physical, in the US especially. There is almost a madness to build the body into sheer muscle. Men building their muscles, through weight-lifting, through running. I think that for many men, this is the quest for the myth of virility.

Menuhin: Yes, but each of these things has a positive aspect. As long as you are working to improve yourself, and not trying to visit your ambitions on others, then you are building self-control. Which can also be led to extremes, but a measure of self-control is a very good thing.

But now, thinking of the third group – the brain and nervous system – that is a kind of control by thought process, by false information, by moulding people's thoughts to what they should think. The big lie! It started out fairly innocently with advertising: *Buy This*, it will cure you of all your ailments. Or: *Buy This*, it will make you grow hair if you are bald. Thought control begins with Freud and psychoanalysis and so on. Everything in human life is like the knife. You could use it to good purpose, you can use it to bad purpose. And psychology can be used to bad purpose. We know that in Russia they used to very recently – or still do – put their dissidents into psychiatric wards because the assumption there is that anyone who doesn't believe in Communism must be wrong. Just as the Christians believe that anyone that does not believe in Christianity must somehow be wrong, be misguided – must even be perhaps evil. One could not be right in the head. Of course, the crazy thing about our dogmatic, fanatical, political ideals is that they can never replace religion, however suspect religion is when practised and organized, when represented by frail men like the old Orthodox Church in Russia, which was corrupt as could be. The less it dealt with the eternal, it dealt with death, with birth, it dealt with eternity. Now Communism doesn't have anything to say about eternity, nothing to say about death, except to be shot by a firing squad. Such a system cannot satisfy people's yearning for things we cannot grasp, things we don't know, and things we have reverence for, or feel a sense of mystery for. Everything to the Communists supposedly is an open book, and they get caught, because life isn't an open book. They can't explain deep necessities. They can't describe man's yearning for the infinite.

Dubal: Have we ever as a human race had to confront more problems than today? For example, the horror of overpopulation. In 1950, Chicago had three million people. In 1990, it still has three million people. In 1950, Mexico City had three million people. But today, it has nearly thirty million people. The world's largest city. It's dying of suffocation. How do we save this city? This has to be attended to right now or a major human population will be dead. It's dying of pollution – no air, no water. They will suffocate in bed.

Menuhin: This is one of the greatest crimes. I knew Mexico City during the war. It was a city where the air was like crystal. The air was like champagne. You lived and walked at 7,000 feet, carried by this marvellous air. We landed there again about eight or nine years ago. You could hardly see two or three yards ahead of you.

Dubal: Let's pretend that I have the power to give you the chance of saving Mexico City – that is now your job. There are now many people who are aware that we are killing the planet. I appoint you to save Mexico City . . .

Menuhin: First of all, we must stop all pollution, that's one thing. We must provide clean water and tents for those who live in filthy slums. It might be necessary to resettle those who would voluntarily want to go to their old haunts they have left in droves for the city, for the attraction of the neon lights. They have lost the attachment to agricultural labour. There is no attachment to the land or responsibility to it, and to the city they go to make their fortunes with no attachments at all – families are gone. The people would have to be reduced to one standard – all the people. As long as the land, the air or water were not clean, all people would have to abide by one standard, including the same food, which would not poison them. The weather is fairly good, so schools could go on outside in tents with good teachers provided, a net of free food and free housing.

Dubal: Free condoms – also the babies must stop. Wombland as Buckminster Fuller called it, is the most dangerous of all zones.

Menuhin: There must be incentives for that. This is a war. But I think that the people who are not from Mexico City can be given land in places where there is little population to make a good life there. To keep the population from multiplying.

Dubal: We are only guests on this planet, and we better teach austerity from the beginning.

Menuhin: This situation will have to happen to survive. But Mexico is still corrupt in its authority and its huge debt. They will never pay it. We must say, 'Forget the debt!' And these conditions have nothing to do with money. 'We absolve you of the debt, but only on these conditions.' Unfortunately, we send in corrupt people. Do we have a body of people we can really trust? Education, housing, morals, ambitions, materialism – all of them fit in together. Each are interrelated. We must make a new awareness as you intimate that this is a global problem.

Dubal: Drugs today are a world-wide disaster. Each of them from alcohol to crack and now *ice* being used to escape despair. Even if they were legalized, the despair wouldn't disappear. It seems like a long time ago in the boiling sixties that some intellectuals like Huxley were enthusiastic about LSD. He once said in an interview in the *Paris Review* of the experience of LSD, he said, 'Many people get tremendous results from mescaline and lysergic acid. Many people get tremendous recalls of buried material and penetrating insights into people around one, and also one's own life – a process which may take six years of psychoanalysis. It happens within an hour and the experience can be very liberating and widening in other ways. It shows that the world one habitually lives in is merely a creation of this conventional, closely conditioned being which one is, and that there are quite other kinds of worlds outside. It's a very salutary thing to realize that the rather dull universe in which most of us spend most of our time is not the only universe there is. I think it's healthy that people should have this experience.'

Menuhin: Very interesting. There was nobody more interesting than Huxley, whom I knew very well. I remember as a child I had frequent ear-aches. In France, a doctor came one day when I was suffering and he used morphine. I shall never forget that bliss, and for years after I longed for it. Though I never had it, I nevertheless realized its power on me. So many people can get hooked on one dose of these drugs and their lives become very different very quickly. It's terrifying. As for the Huxley idea, this came at a time when they couldn't foresee the exaggeration and the great dangers. In the beginning, one only sees the promise and does not see the rather perverse fulfilment of this indulgence. I'd rather take the six years or twelve years of searching. I don't believe in short cuts whereby something is used. That eliminates the process and gives you the final sensation. This is an impoverishment, because it is the process of getting there which is the real satisfaction. If you have to tussle with yourself, search for yourself, to discover yourself, if you have to search out other modes of existence, if you come to the conclusion that there must be other forms of consciousness that you must experience. I don't want it done for me by a drug or by a pleasure electrode. I resent being manipulated – I can't bear it – by a demagogue, or music coming through musak, or anything trying to make me feel one way or another, from docile to irritated. I like my existence. I like the combination of the sensual, intellectual, the spiritual, I'm fortunately not under pressure to find escapes through a drug. I can't really share the world of those who must find some escape.

Dubal: Of course, Huxley already knew that he wasn't writing any novels under LSD. It's a colour dream, a visual world. But it held so many in thrall, and one could understand the thrill and even hope it once held for some.

Menuhin: Oh yes, definitely. As Huxley said, there are other realms. But we are trapped in bodies. The need to escape is so understandable. Millions of us lead such frustrating dull lives and who find no reasons to live. There are perhaps many of us trapped in unlikely bodies. For instance, the Romeo trapped in an ungainly hulk.

Dubal: Yes, this too is so interesting – what we really are within and what we look like. The two don't always match well. Look at Gieseking, a huge creature, playing Debussy on a puff of air. Somerset Maugham once wrote that 'I think many people shrink from the notion that the body can have an effect on the constitution of the soul. There is nothing of which for my part I am more assured. My soul would have been quite different if I had not stammered or if I had been four or five inches taller.'

Menuhin: How absolutely fascinating and true. Each pair of hands make for a different violinist.

Dubal: Look at the musical talent locked away in hands that are too big or too small. Some just cannot sing through their fingers.

Menuhin: Yes, one's worldly existence can at times feel like a shell for what you are inside of you. As a child I often saw myself totally detached from myself. There is this capacity for detachment and separation of elements which we push too far while we are looking for a *particular* state of being.

Dubal: Humankind has many drives, we are propelled by tremendous forces. Good and evil – life and death – the more we study ourselves, the more complex the human race appears. What is one of the chief drives in your estimation?

Menuhin: Most certainly the drive for continuity: we want continuity and desperately – that is what we are *made* for. And the ecstasy of creation, which many people know in terms of basic procreation, is part of the mystic union with the infinite which we deeply desire, and thirst for. When the artist achieves a great creation, all of this is part of the same drive of life to see itself renewed. It's self-expression, but it's even deeper than that. It's more than self-expression; it's part of a general drive. I feel there is a progression that we recognize, but once we try to put it into words it defeats us. The progression from bad to better. We *do* know what is better. We do know a smiling child is better than a battered child. We do know that, we do know a beautiful poem is better than something growled out by a drill sergeant. There is progression, and the progression between the perfect gesture, or the perfect phrasing, or the perfect movement of an acrobat or dancer, *is* better than the gesture of someone who is about to fall off the road.

Dubal: And we know that – and we feel it very early in our lives.

Menuhin: Very early – yes. Yes, a child is driven by that – they handle a thing and are looking for ways to handle it which are more economical, more direct, more purposeful, more elegant. When we see something which is ugly, why do we call it ugly? Because it's not harmonious. We recognize it early. We have in us a direction of evolution. If we write we are looking for good syntax. Why this passion for the Olympic Games? Because we want to see the highest form of what we are doing – riding horses, running, jumping, skating. We see, every day, people, watching as I do, and all united with these perfect runners, and these marvellous athletes. It started with the Greeks, and of course even earlier. The quest for transcendence, it's something we all live for.

Dubal: Yes, for a hundred years runners were trying to break the barrier of the four-minute mile; finally in the 1950s, Roger Bannister, I believe, ran something like 3:59.8, and it was quickly followed by John Landy – and now it's commonplace.

Menuhin: It's extraordinary. We are driven by this, but so much of it unfortunately is vicarious today. Passivity today is terrible, and I believe unprecedented. We watch television, munching on these poisonous pizzas, as we see every kind and nuance of violence. This kind of dichotomy between what is watched and what is experienced is dangerous. There is a difference between living it and seeing it, and being part of it and being part of the misery and the terror. You don't get an unhealthy mind living reality. The soul does not sink. One may confront reality. One can become stronger. Look at Dostoevsky – Siberia didn't destroy him. The terrible business is seeing it, even in bright colour, yet not being part of it. Children can *read* fairy tales, even Grimm's, which are pretty grim. But it doesn't matter as long as they read them, and as long as they don't have the visual tangible image. They make their own image. As long as you read them, they will never affect your mind negatively. But if you translate them into film, and see them as we would reality – the blood and the gore and so on – that is a totally different dimension.

Dubal: Yes, but the young today are enraptured with films of horror. They applaud, they scream, they want to be frightened. It's as if they are getting themselves ready to experience the sub-human.

Menuhin: Yes, I know, it's unbelievable. I feel a progressive alienation.

Dubal: Yes! That's the word. The original definition of the word 'alien' means insane.

Menuhin: When I was a boy, the delivery boy, whatever he brought on his bicycle, might whistle or might sing, and the boy selling newspapers would often sing something. That all seems almost gone today. Oh, about thirty years ago on a very hot day in Philadelphia I was walking through a slum district, and there were actually people sitting outside their homes, singing. That is apparently gone today.

Dubal: It's again the active and the passive. Today people will blast your senses with their horrid radios. Spitting out the endless, mindless beat of bad rock music.

Menuhin: Last night we had a late supper with Slava [Rostropovich]. We came out on the street in Georgetown; none of the people did I want to stop and ask something of, or even speak to.

Dubal: Are you joking? They could murder you without feeling any remorse. That is alienation. Murder is unreal today. It's on every TV show. Murder in America is a gruesome fact of life. Cities here are all dangerous. They each have their 'combat zones'.

Menuhin: Well, that is a sad, sad thing. When I was a boy you could walk on the streets. Even in New York, during the war, when New York was the greatest, most important city in the world. But now it's too late.

Dubal: Yes, it's too late. I once loved New York, but I can't love it anymore. It's getting worse every day. Talk about alienation, you can't even walk a block. The homeless out there are not singing. Each month they are out on those streets talking to themselves, which breeds a terrible insanity. The deterioration in five years in Manhattan is hardly to be believed. There must be 200,000 homeless in Manhattan alone.

Menuhin: Yes, the world is coming to our door. Look at the Chinese making their Statue of Liberty. How touching. They want to emulate us. And now what do we have to offer them? I think we had better come to our senses, and spell out what we stand for in the world.

Dubal: Well, we stand for nothing much, I'm afraid – for a very decadent capitalism, which raises money as its only ideal. Newspaper headlines telling us 'The Best Sex Donald Trump Ever Had'. The marketing of junk and more junk. I wish Thoreau could for one day emerge from Walden Pond and walk the streets of New York. He would think he'd be in hell's fantasy. Thoreau, the man who wrote in his essay, 'Life Without Principle', 'The ways by which you may get money almost without exception lead downward. To have done anything by which you earned money *merely* is to have been truly idle or worse.' I know you see many young people – some of the very best. They are soft. They are concerned with our dying planet. Some even write poetry. How are they going to protect themselves without becoming numb – by staying alert, and even vulnerable. They have to protect themselves, and they don't know how.

Menuhin: They don't know how, you are absolutely right. But I think they must, within the measure of their possibilities, try to choose well, whatever it is they have to choose – opinions or food. If they have a choice. But they cannot succumb to total despair, by being in a sense naïvely idealistic. For instance, by understanding that being non-violent, one can bring about something better. But there has to be a measure of self-protection. People must learn to do and understand two things at the same time. Either they are pacifists, or they are the opposite and are aggressive and feel that it's one way. The greater Israel, or the greater Brazil, or whatever it is. But it's the balance we need. A measure of wisdom, a measure of determination, a measure of sophistication, of accepting what is not going to easily be changed, but to try best to change what you can, together with others all over the world. All this exists in embryo. There are young people who care.

Dubal: Yes, but the embryo is crushed quickly – often

ruthlessly. I'm afraid part of the human brain is defective, the part that is split and mentally sick is getting the upper hand, especially with a world population that is already four billion too many.

Menuhin: The ancient legend of the Garden of Eden, and the insidious poison of knowledge, has a great truth in it. Man is madder than animals by virtue of his reason and self-consciousness, and his ability to remember and to imagine and to project. We direct our earthly life according to an image, either contained in words, or contained in a vision or commitment, or whatever it may be. Patriotic, or idealistic. Now we don't even have that. We have violence for violence's sake.

Dubal: Once we had good manners, which stopped much violence in the early stages –

Menuhin: Yes, as you say, good manners. Courtesy, which was once thought to be hypocritical, turns out to have been a very useful lubrication of society. The fact that we lead our lives according to an ideal is already a form of madness, because we allow our everyday decisions to be determined by a totally improbable, intangible motto or principle, however we have clothed it. But actually that motto or principle is used, very often, to justify what we want to do anyway. So we put up the flag to extol whatever we want to give a false nobility.

Dubal: What is a good sign of our era?

Menuhin: One thing, many people have at least shed naïve beliefs in 'isms' altogether – Fascism, Communism, Capital-ism – and the more we do that, the better.

Dubal: How do you handle the world of today, this deeply sorrowful time?

Menuhin: I'm very fortunate: I have music; I have a marvellous wife; I had marvellous parents who gave complete devotion as well as fidelity to each other. I have marvellous children, none of them drug-takers or alcoholics. I have great satisfactions: when I conduct great orchestras, when I visit my school, when I see the returns I get from this school, the people who come back to see me after concerts. Somehow I followed every opportunity I had. So much has been returned to me. Yet I well know there is a new generation which has grown up, which I have no contact with at all. Those are the people I saw in the streets of Georgetown, or even the young people at concerts, who come out into the world with poor education, sort of a bit unhealthy, not very clear in the head. They are products of a civilization that offers ready-made solutions. So they can handle their computer things, but they can only handle instruments that already know the information and probably know the answer. If you asked them, 'What seat do do I have on the plane?' they can touch their keys and tell you exactly.

Dubal: The computer is a devil. It will alienate people more than ever. These machines that so many people automatically swear by that make life 'easier'.

Menuhin: Exactly. The problem is, if you ask many people for their own opinion, they may have none. And if they have a conviction, they don't know now how to go about it, to implement it. They re unaccustomed to formulating a plan. But in my case, I am shielded. I am very fortunate. I can talk to you, or the other day Helmut Schmidt turned up after a concert and we talked till 2 a.m. I feel an obligation because I am so fortunate, to do what little I can in propagating something that is positive. And I have music, the pursuit of music.

Dubal: Well, I continue here to be the devil's advocate –

music has become a madness. At the rate junk music is pro-
liferating, it will wipe out the art of music as you know it.
There is very little sensibility left to cultivate fine music. You
can't escape music. And the incredible thing, it's this very
junk music, this primitive under-beat, that keeps people
halfway alive. For millions, music is all they have and it
keeps them sane. There is one song with the title, 'When I
Get to Heaven Will There Still Be Rock 'n' Roll?' And then
music being forced to be part of commercials – Pavlov and
Orpheus in deadly alliance.

Menuhin: Yes, rock 'n' roll has grown to epidemic proportions.

Dubal: Is this what we have from the democratization of the
world – and all that man has suffered – he is imprisoned by
the addiction of rock 'n' roll, day and night through walls?
Michael Jackson has sold more 'units' of one abominable
song than all the violinists in history. And do you watch the
TV commercials?

Menuhin: Yes, advertisements depict countrysides that are
more green than anything you can see in reality. All with
happy people, fishing, or lying under palm trees.

Dubal: It's horrible, sentimental, the nostalgia industry.
It's all part of the marketing mentality. There's no green
left. The size of one football field every second is destroyed
in the Amazon rain forests. They are the 'developers', which
is really another word for destroyers. All these forests
felled so cattle can graze on open land to sell more cheap
hamburgers.

Menuhin: I know – I know it's out of control. In my own
lifetime, I can recall Ireland; when I first went, there was
an indescribable green. The kind of green that you only
get now in artificial colouring – like Technicolour. One sees
the dryness of the soil everywhere as a result of the use of
fertilizers.

Dubal: Do you ever hear rock 'n' roll?

Menuhin: Not intentionally, but you can't escape this popular music, or indeed much other music. You know, rock 'n' roll is frightening because it is part of the mob mind feeding the desire of a large group of people to escape from reality.

Dubal: It is as potent and as dangerous as any drug. Mick Jagger or Michael Jackson leading an army . . .

Menuhin: I once was in the situation of being at a rock concert. The music, if such a word can be used, was torture for me. The sheer volume of sound was overwhelming, and my self-composure was vanishing. I had to resist, to remain true to myself. Everything is calculated to dominate one's senses. I was unable to participate in this commercialization, this contrived, depersonalizing, cheap hysteria. Thousands of pounds had been spent on sets and lighting, the group wore clothes covered with rhinestones and sequins, which hurt the eyes as they reflected the light. The look of the young people was hypnotized. If they could have known my feelings they would have booed me and said I didn't understand them or their pleasure or their needs. What they didn't realize was that they were in a serious condition of being manipulated. It was disturbing to see all these young people so numbed, imitating the gestures of the group on stage, their emotions being taunted for commercial gain.

Dubal: The musicalization of the world through rock is one of the frightening things of our time. This is no longer the sweet Beatles in Liverpool. We are prisoners of rock 'n' roll. There is an ad on TV that says rock 'n' roll will live forever.

Menuhin: This is far from the Beatles' beginnings, originating spontaneously, in the small streets of Liverpool.

Dubal: Do you think the twentieth century, with its slogans of progress and education, with its cruelty and devastation, has been a better or worse time to live generally? For instance, would you have preferred to live in eighteenth-century France?

Menuhin: No, I would not have preferred that. I think our century offers such excitement, such diversity of opportunity. It's a century that has established degrees between kinds, rather than absolute differences. I always compare it with the states of gas, water and ice. They do turn at definite temperatures into different things. We know more about degrees. Unlike our ancestors, we are no longer as certain about many things: we are no longer sure of good and evil, black and white. In a way, it's a healthy thing – we now see how things can change gradually. We are really very uncertain of our bearings. We now have to find a new compass. The morality will not change. The great seers will be reinvested with a new sacredness if we find our way in the new directions which are upon us. But of course we are living in an insecure, interim period between old certainties and new certainties. The web that binds human beings in a community, these webs, many of them have dissolved, and people are more isolated than they ever have been before.

Dubal: A person of the Middle Ages felt no alienation. He was certain the world was flat. He was certain of his God. He never travelled beyond his village where he felt secure.

Menuhin: I'm sure that in the tiny island of Manhattan, with its millions of souls, there is a great number who live lives that are not attached lovingly to families or other helpful supporting webs, I would call them. This is a very great tragedy. We have to relearn our relationship with all of life. We cannot live isolated existences, neither as human beings nor as nations nor as races nor as religions. Therefore we must begin to cultivate these ties, these links. We naturally

feel sad when great tracts of land and beautiful trees are
destroyed. We naturally feel sad when millions of people are
dying of famine, or that mobs of people go off their heads –
and rave and kill. These are aspects of man's madness – this
shows that our thinking faculty is not coupled with our universal, sensitive, intuitive and compassionate nature. We
grab at solutions. Because we cannot compare them with the
past, we are like new-born people.

Today the young mother is given all sorts of reading material
on how to raise a child. In the past, when traditions existed,
when the food was established, when the family existed and
when no new elements existed in society, the mother didn't
have to learn how to raise and care for the child. But today
the young mother is isolated in generations and isolated from
other community mothers. Very often not wanting the child
and unable to look after the child. All of this is a sign of great
alienation – alienation from the earth and the air. I think young
people are more aware of this than ever before, and bringing
the older ones into line.

Dubal: I think that the *young* are more alienated and isolated
than ever before. The amazing amount of babies born out
of wedlock, as they say, is staggering. Young girls fourteen
years old desperately wanting something of their own to love,
bring babies into the world by the thousands a month in the
US alone. They can't begin to handle them, and adolescents
soon lose all faith in life. I don't see much awareness of the
young today, such as say in the 1960s. Even the so-called
educated young today are proving to be incompetent in their
professions. They live for money. A few labels on cigarettes
or foodstuffs means almost nothing. No, I see less awareness
than ever before – and more and more gluttony. Everything,
every species, is endangered. The cheetah and the jaguar –
certainly more beautiful than we are – have only a few years
on this planet. No, I think that you hold on to those few

who you see who tell you that in their fields they are showing awareness for the human situation. But really you must take a walk with me in any city in the US and talk to the millions of hopeless blacks, Hispanics, drug addicts and homeless. Believe me, not the American depression, nothing equals the general despair of the present. And there will be no non-violent Martin Luther King any longer, or a Gandhi. The blacks are arming, and I fear TV and Madison Avenue along with the orgy of rock music, and the lack of these webs and links as you call them, will produce, especially in the US, a devastating tension on the streets. Just driving an automobile in this country shows you the aggressive tension that never stops – it's a battlefield on the highways. As for Europe, their values of freedom will be the new car, the endless products. I fear a new fascism in Europe, not a United Europe. As for Central and South America, as for the Middle East, as for the avaricious values of Japan and Korea – one commentator said the average American is today a mystic dreamer compared to the average Asian. No, you have been one of the more fortunate beings of our century, and you have given us freely and bounteously of your art and your love; but you must recruit a whole army of Menuhins to stave off the wolf in us.

Menuhin: Yes, yes, the catastrophe is right around the corner. There used to be endless time; now time has shrunk, time has taken the rays into its own destiny. We are now having less and less influence on our destiny. Far from achieving mastery of nature. It seems like mastery when we go to the moon. But the time factor is the crucial one. Do we have the time to educate ourselves into the awareness you plead for? That is the great question.

Dubal: Yes, Erich Fromm said, 'Man can be human only in a climate in which he can expect that he and his children will live to see the next year and many more years to come.' The human race is not only starving but more and more in pyscho-logical pain.

Menuhin: I don't see what will save us. Yet I see many marvel-lous human beings who see the right thing and do the right things.

Dubal: Yes, but they are constantly crushed. We are happy to talk about a few less bombs. Why do we even permit arma-ments?

Menuhin: Yes, they are crushed. There is no great movement aloft. You are perfectly right, there must now be a totally new form of dialogue. We have seen now the dangers of the capitalistic system in its present manifestation, a marvellous system enabling the growth of great individuality, initiative, dynamic power, freedom to achieve, all with great risk. The risk factor that we have in the US is one of the highest in the world. But the dynamic aspect of what can be done in every field – science, medicine, art, architecture – is quite astound-ing as compared to the choked societies of Russia and the Eastern countries. But the danger of today in post-indust-rialist society is isolation and great loneliness of spirit. The machine has made us into crumbs. Our taste buds have been debased – sugar is in almost everything. Americans are like machines – and take what the machines give them. Food and drink, for instance, is never an arm's length away.

Dubal: We must fight bitterly to retain our humanness. Adlai Stevenson once said, 'He didn't fear so much anymore men becoming slaves, he feared us becoming robots.'

Index